FORECAST
YOUR FUTURE

AN ASTROLOGICAL GUIDE
FOR THE TEN YEARS

2021–2030

PETER WEST

GREEN MAGIC

Green Magic
Seed Factory
Aller
Langport
Somerset
TA10 0QN
England

www.greenmagicpublishing.com

Typeset by K.DESIGN
Winscombe, Somerset

ISBN 9781838132439

GREEN MAGIC

Contents

The Natural Zodiac

(Midheaven)

(Ascendant)

Symbols, Glyphs and Abbreviations

Signs of the Zodiac

Aries	♈	Leo	♌	Sagittarius	♐
Taurus	♉	Virgo	♍	Capricorn	♑
Gemini	♊	Libra	♎	Aquarius	♒
Cancer	♋	Scorpio	♏	Pisces	♓

Planets

Sun	☉	Moon	☽	Mercury	☿
Venus	♀	Mars	♂	Jupiter	♃
Saturn	♄	Uranus	♅	Neptune	♆
		Pluto	♇		

"The Natural Zodiac"

CHAPTER ONE

Basic Astrology

Traditionally, it has always been considered that astrology is concerned with the relationships between the heavenly bodies and the events that occur here on Earth.

The Zodiac

Once every year, the Earth travels round the Sun, and each of the remaining planets – Mercury, Venus, Mars, Jupiter, Saturn, Uranus, Neptune and Pluto – follow in their individual paths in much the same orbit or plane. This plane is technically called the 'ecliptic' and is a belt, or pathway, through the heavens. The more popular name for this orbital phenomenon is the zodiac or the pathway of the animals. It is divided in to twelve separate sections known as the signs.

Most of us know these signs as Aries, the Ram; Taurus, the Bull; Gemini, the Twins; Cancer, the Crab; Leo, the Lion; Virgo, the Maiden; Libra, the Scales; Scorpio, the Scorpion; Sagittarius, the Archer; Capricorn the Goat; Aquarius, the Water Carrier and Pisces, the Fish.

Each sign has a correspondence with a planet or planets. Each of these planets is said to "rule" that sign, the people born during the time the Sun passes thought it and everything else associated with it. Thus, everything has an affiliation in some way, with one or, possibly, more signs and planets because in a couple of very special cases there are what is known as "dual" rulerships. This is because modern astrologers have concluded that certain of the older rulerships assigned many centuries ago are now out of date. The newly discovered planets seem to have better affinities with certain signs, areas and circumstances and so they have taken their place in the modern order of things.

Such changes are continuously on-going and made from what has been discovered and accepted throughout the years – a natural progression in any study. People born as the Sun transits, or passes through a sign as it does once a year are called after that sign. Thus, a Sun-Aries or Sun-Taurus person is someone born when the Sun passed through Aries or Taurus respectively. These subjects are more colloquially known as an Arian or a Taurean and so on. The Sun enters and transits (or passes though) each sign at a slightly different time from year to year.

This is because astrologers use astronomical, civil or clock time. The exact time at which the Sun, Moon and planets enter the signs for any year is given in an ephemeris – a publication which shows all the relevant astronomical and astrological data for any year. They are published for varying time spans as annuals or for ten, fifty or even a hundred years in advance. Some are set for 00.00 hours midnight and some at 12.00 hours noon.

The Signs of the Zodiac

The most generally accepted dates for the entry of the Sun into each of the signs together with the planets said to rule them are shown in this table:

SIGN	ENTRY DATE	RULER
Aries	21 March	Mars
Taurus	20 April	Venus
Gemini	20 April	Mercury
Cancer	22 June	Moon
Leo	23 July	Sun
Virgo	23 August	Mercury
Libra	23 September	Venus

SIGN	ENTRY DATE	RULER
Scorpio	23 October	Pluto
Sagittarius	22 November	Jupiter
Capricorn	22 December	Saturn
Aquarius	20 January	Uranus
Pisces	19 February	Neptune

The dividing line between any two signs is called the cusp and has led to the expression 'I am cusp-born'. It can be seen that anyone born very late in one sign or very early in the next would need an ephemeris to determine the place of the Sun (or any other planet for that matter) on their birthday. For example, all people born on May 20 2016 would need to do this because on that day the Sun left Taurus to enter Gemini at 14.36 hours. Those born before the change would be classified as Taureans while those born after would be Geminians.

The Types of Signs

Each of the astrological signs belongs to two different basic groups. These are the quadruplicities or qualities each of which are linked with our leadership abilities and activity levels along with the triplicities or elements which are concerned mostly with feelings and emotional responses.

The quadruplicities are in three groups of four signs: cardinal, fixed and mutable. The cardinal signs are Aries, Cancer, Libra and Capricorn. People born in these signs will always demonstrate leadership qualities one way or the other and for good or ill. They are always ready to direct, take the lead and make decisions as prevailing circumstances dictate. These people are very much outgoing types.

The fixed signs are Taurus, Leo, Scorpio and Aquarius and as the name suggests those born in this group are rather fixed in their ways. They are rather determined, persistent and stubborn but generally regarded as stable personalities.

The mutable signs are Gemini, Virgo, Sagittarius and Pisces. The people born in this group are clever, flexible and adaptable.

As a rule they seem to have a knack of 'knowing' what is going on around them and they bend with the wind accordingly. They are mostly obliging characters.

There are four triplicities and they represent the elements of Fire, Earth, Air and Water. Each section contains three signs.

Aries, Leo and Sagittarius are theFire signs. People born during these periods are always active in some way and generally tend to possess good leadership qualities. They have lively but rather impatient personalities.

Taurus, Virgo and Capricorn are the Earth signs. As a rule they are practical and full of common sense when dealing with problems especially when faced with immediate or necessary decisions. They are rather down-to-earth folk.

The Air signs are Gemini, Libra and Aquarius. These people almost always have good communication skills and are socially orientated, clever and intellectually perceptive. Among this group you will find the 'ideas' people.

Cancer, Scorpio and Pisces are the Water signs. Those born in this group tend to 'feel' their way through life because they always seem to appreciate the emotional needs of those around them. They are sensitive and receptive personalities.

The twelve Sun-signs are also further divided into masculine or positive signs and feminine or negative signs. The odd numbered signs, Aries, Gemini, Leo, Libra, Sagittarius and Aquarius are termed positive signs for these people are on average more assertive and self-expressive. The remaining six, Taurus, Cancer, Virgo, Scorpio, Capricorn and Pisces are the negative signs. People born as the Sun is passing through them are less assertive and inclined to be slightly self-repressive.

The terms positive and negative are meant in their astrological interpretation and might be better understood as male and female respectively but not in the more usually accepted sense.

As you read this you might well have already begun to recognise a part of the behaviour patterns of colleagues, close friends and relatives. However, astrology is not that straightforward. You need to know a little more about how it all works. For example, the short interpretation for each of the Sun-signs just given is based on the period when the Sun is passing through a particular sign. There is no allowance for the influence of the Moon or any of the other planets being in that sign at the same time as the Sun, or indeed anywhere else in the zodiac for that matter.

The Aspects

No account has been made so far for the angular relationships, or aspects, that occur between the planets. Some are very important and rather special, but once again, what they represent and how they should be interpreted is left entirely to the astrologer and his (or her) personal preferences.

As the Sun, Moon and planets pursue their individual paths along the ecliptic they occasionally form an angle or series of angles to each other. When the horoscope is drawn up, angles like this or a series of angles may be formed from these planets to major points of the chart. There are a great many of them. Some are natural and some are man-made. That is to say, planetary, or mutual aspects that occur in the heavens are natural, while those to various points of a birth chart are man-made.

Astronomically, all aspects are defined angular distances and because they are viewed from the Earth they are called geocentric aspects. There are four major aspects: 0, 90, 120 and 180 degrees, otherwise known as the conjunction, square, trine and opposition respectively. There are also a wide number of other angular positions of much lesser importance. For an astrologer, to be able to understand and interpret them is very important. They qualify and quantify the relative strengths and weaknesses in their relationships to one another in addition to their basic house and sign position that chart.

The birth chart represents a 360 degree picture of the heavens so that all the angles that are formed are as a result of the circle being divided by a number. Traditionally, aspects have always been divided into good or bad, hard or soft or easy or difficult types. For example, the 180 degree opposition angle, created when the circle is divided by 2, is regarded as stressful, creating tension and making life a little difficult. If you stop and think about it for a moment, two or more bodies opposing one another does suggest that some kind of conflict is involved.

The conjunction, that is when two or more planets are located next to each other, suggests their combined energies are likely to become quite concentrated because of their proximity. And so it is with all of the other aspects. In the last twenty years or so one of the previously considered minor aspects, the inconjunct, or quincunx aspect of 150 degrees has become the object of a lot of study. It is now much more widely used and almost always indicates a stressful attitude. Many modern astrologers are of the opinion that this link may be connected with workplace and or health issues. But perhaps a tad more to the point this angle is now regarded as a major aspect and is the subject of several published books.

And, as we have advanced astrologers will look to see whether (most) aspects are recorded as approaching, exact or departing. An approaching aspect is when two or more planets are sufficiently close to one another to be regarded as being in aspect. The aspect become exact when they do finally meet, and a departing aspect is so-called as they begin to pull away from each other's influence.

Try to imagine yourself on your own waiting for a train on a platform in an underground station. Shortly before it arrives you will feel a slight breeze that grows as the train pushes the air in front of it. The nearer it approaches the stronger this rush of air will be. A little later the rails begin to "sing" and, suddenly, as the train roars into the station all and sundry experience the effect. Then, after a few minutes, the doors close, and the train departs as suddenly as it arrived.

Once it has gone all is quiet again. This effect is rather similar to a planetary aspect as it begins to form, becomes exact and then moves out of orb again. This illustrates that an aspect does not have to be exact for at least some of its effects to be felt. This is especially so when assessing aspects in progressions and transits.

The allowable distance for an approaching or departing aspect is called an orb. Therefore, the closer the orb, the more influence is exerted by the planets involved. The wider apart they are, the less effect they have on each other. Opinions have always differed as to the degree of orb allowable and it is left entirely to the individual astrologer. In addition to these major aspects, you must remember there are also a number of minor ones. If too wide an orb is allowed for a major aspect, it might easily encroach on or hide a minor one.

Some astrologers may use all of the aspects; others are just as likely to ignore some. It is all left to the personal taste of the individual. But either way, these aspects have an influence on the character and personality of the person or matter under review. Here, I would like to place on record that my own preferences are to allow only tight (closer) orbs for aspects. One of the many reasons there are very few so-called "pure" Sun-sign types is probably because some astrologers tend to allow for the orb of an aspect to be rather wide.

The continuous interplay of the planets with each other detracts from the purity of any Sun-sign personality. Having explained the interplay of all the different aspects, places and positions that the planets occupy together with their influence on each other, the astrologer must also take note whether each planet does or does not make or receive aspects.

To be able to understand all this information properly it has to be collected into one place: the horoscope or birth chart. A horoscope (horo + scope: hour + picture) is really a picture of the heavens at the exact moment of birth or for the event you want to investigate. It is the focal point for the vast majority of astrological calculations and interpretations.

For a chart to be exact you need to have the precise moment of birth – year, month, day and time – preferably to within four minutes. You will have to give the astrologer the exact location for him (or her) to determine its longitude and latitude. If you were born in a remote place you ought to include the nearest large town or city. From this data the astrologer will calculate your personal horoscope.

There are quite a few ways of achieving this. An astrologer may use a computer or draw the chart by hand. He or she may record some or all of the planetary positions and their individual relationships to each other, or just those they think are the most relevant.

Astrology is neither an art nor a science: it is both. All the calculations and mechanics of the scientific side are synthesised together with the technique(s) employed in the interpretation. Together, they produce a study of people, or an insight into the events or other matters for which the horoscope was raised. Thus, I consider it an art-science.

The Sun, Moon and planets have varying strengths and weaknesses that are dependent on where they appear in a chart. Further, the actual chart itself has focal points in terms of interpretation and meaning. There are so many different factors to take into account it is easy to understand why some readings and opinions can differ so greatly.

If you were to commission seven astrologers to make a horoscope from the same basic information, each would look at the subject from their personal point of view. It would be the same as putting seven photographers in a studio. Each of them would see the subject matter from their personal point of view and the results would reflect this. They would take their photograph as they interpret not only what they see but also how they see it.

To demonstrate this more fully, and to take the matter that one stage further let us look at three people each born with the Sun in Cancer but who all seem to exhibit quite different characteristics. If the first person also had the Moon in Cancer then he will be rather sensitive, a trifle diffident at times and would be well known for his belief in the traditional way doing things.

If the second person had the Moon in Virgo he would display a marked critical nature but would always be courteous and tactful in his dealings with everyone. If the third Sun-Cancerian had the Moon in Capricorn, one would expect to find a practical and ambitious nature perhaps a tad too cautious at times but also a realist at heart.

Three quite different Cancer subjects so that when the time comes for you to judge the chart after you have placed Mercury, Venus and the rest of the other planets you will see how these heavenly bodies exert their different and quite individual influences in their special way. So, if two people have the Sun in Scorpio and the Moon in Gemini but with the planet Mars in yet another different sign, then the influence of that planet will reflect the differences.

Astrologers use ten planets, twelve signs and twelve houses, four major aspects and, literally, a whole host of other minor influences that ought to be but are not always taken into account every time an astrologer judges a chart. So, when the planets and other features of a birth chart together with all the individual and relative positions are taken into account then the whole picture changes – often considerably.

The Sun, Moon and Planets

To illustrate this better here is a brief interpretation of the varying strengths and weaknesses of the Sun, Moon and planets.

The Sun

The power house of our system, the giver of life, the prime mover and major influence of all we think and do, the Sun is perhaps the most important feature of the birth chart. It shows our most essential personality tempered by its position in the chart. It is the symbol of our personal well-being and shows the way we need to express ourselves. Sometimes, dependent on its placing in the chart it could be difficult to trace this properly because there are positive and negative vibrations to decipher and translate. These are based on where the Sun is in a chart, its relationships or aspects with any other planet or planets and the various parts of the birth chart. It is the same for all the other heavenly bodies.

The Moon

In essence, the Moon has no real power of her own. She influences our emotional response of the moment, our instinctive reactions to whatever situation we find ourselves in. Think of a chameleon when considering her as she reflects these influences.

Mercury

The first planet from the Sun influences communication of all kinds. How we think and reason, calculate and then decide on a subsequent course of action depends on where Mercury is placed in the chart. It rules our basic instincts, our urge to gain knowledge and then how we use or pass on that information.

Venus

The second planet from the Sun reveals how we react emotionally, socially and artistically. She conditions our tastes, appearance and style of dress. She also indicates how we will (might) react when people or things let us down. Our artistic appreciation is conditioned and shaped by the position of this planet.

Mars

This planet influences our physical energy levels and the way we assert ourselves. Our initiative and resistance and how we direct those impulses are also shown. Often, we can determine what the subject wants from life by how he or she adopts and adapts to their social position to achieve their aims.

Jupiter

We look to this planet to ascertain our moral and ethical nature, our sense of purpose and how we seek to improve ourselves as we progress. Our compassion and generosity levels are also shown.

It also influences the way we use opportunity to further personal ambition and establish our position in society.

Saturn

This planet influences our level of personal responsibility and discipline, how we acquire them and live within the restrictions imposed by our sense of limitation. It also shows how we may best find order and security within these parameters. Perseverance can take us beyond these limits when or if we condition ourselves to do so.

Uranus

This body shows our creative sense and how we express ourselves. When we fail to follow convention it usually reveals our inner, (naturally) rebellious streak showing how we break free to seek new experiences and how to justify these actions. The inclination to reform established practices is rarely far from the surface.

Neptune

This planet influences the way we choose to experience our needs, wants, dreams and fantasies. Its position in the birth chart will also show how we tend to deceive not only ourselves but others in the pursuit of these ideals. Our ego and emotional stability may also be conditioned here. If we need to improve our experience of real life we should look to this planet first for it may not always be a practical influence.

Pluto

While Pluto may have been downgraded in that it is no longer recognised as a planet, it is still used by astrologers and it governs or indicates our innermost convictions and compulsions. The desire to control, take or even seize power is also shown here.

How this may be achieved is conditioned by what we may have had to give up first. In essence, how we effect such a transformation is related directly to what are considered to be conventional or normal behavioural patterns for this may not always be the right way.

The Houses

Today, the modern astrologer has a wide choice of house division methods that he or she can use to create a birth chart. In all, there are more than a dozen, but it is not within the scope of this work to delve into and explain all the mathematical intricacies involved in astrological house division.

As a rule, most astrologers tend to use the Equal House system. Whatever the arguments may be for or against any of the others it is widely accepted that this is the easiest to use and understand. Therefore, all the following house meanings and explanations are based on this system.

Birth charts are divided into twelve segments or houses and each house has its own meaning that is roughly equivalent to a sign of the zodiac. Each house will have a sign on its cusp or beginning as the chart is created. Aries, the first sign of the zodiac may be said to be the same as the first house while Taurus corresponds with the second house; Gemini, the third; Cancer, the fourth and so on to Pisces, the natural twelfth house.

So, for example, Cancer, the fourth sign of the zodiac is said to be more powerfully placed if it should fall into the fourth house for this house corresponds to Cancer in the natural order of the zodiac. Now, in some cases the position of a planet may create a dual correspondence between a house and a sign. As the Earth travels on its daily path around the Sun, the signs are seen to move through the houses at varying speeds.

Thus, at any one time, one of these signs will be on the first house cusp. This part of the chart and in particular, the degree of that sign is called the Ascendant and astrologers everywhere regard this as a very special point in a horoscope.

The Ascendant, the whole of that house and each subsequent

one has an affinity with certain areas of life. Planets and signs fall within the influence of a house according to their position in the horoscope. Mostly, the meanings of the houses are a traditional matter, but these days they are also tempered by the experience of the astrologer concerned and the results of modern research. Each of the houses relate by polarity. The first house is linked with the seventh while the second relate to the eighth and so on all the way round.

As houses are merely the places of the planets they are normally referred to by the number sequence from one (1) through to twelve (12). This is unlike the signs, all of which are known by their individual name(s). The houses and the signs do have some correspondence in that the first house roughly equates with the first sign, Aries; the second house with the second sign, Taurus, and so on.

Thus:

House 1	corresponds with or is equal to	Aries
House 2	corresponds with or is equal to	Taurus
House 3	corresponds with or is equal to	Gemini
House 4	corresponds with or is equal to	Cancer
House 5	corresponds with or is equal to	Leo
House 6	corresponds with or is equal to	Virgo
House 7	corresponds with or is equal to	Libra
House 8	corresponds with or is equal to	Scorpio
House 9	corresponds with or is equal to	Sagittarius
House 10	corresponds with or is equal to	Capricorn
House 11	corresponds with or is equal to	Aquarius
House 12	corresponds with or is equal to	Pisces

This sequence remains constant at all times when we employ the Equal House chart system. Each of the houses relates by polarity. Thus, the first house is linked with the seventh, while the second relates to the eighth, and so on, all the way round the zodiac and the chart. As you read through these explanations you will notice these relationships become more apparent.

The First House

This indicates our basic personality, how we would prefer the world to see us and the steps that we actually take to ensure this usually remains fairly constant but that would be according to the planets in the house, if any, of course. Our general disposition, vitality, temperament and how we look physically is also largely governed from this house.

The sign on the cusp, its ruling planet or the planet or planets in the house wield an extremely strong influence on our physical well-being and overall behavioural patterns throughout our life. In many cases, planets here can often prove to be more influential than the Sun sign, which for most astrologers is often the most important part of the horoscope.

The Second House

This house shows how we relate to our income and expenditure along with material possessions and overall response to our financial needs, wants, personal security and in many cases, our feelings and emotions connected with these matters. The reader should be reminded that this refers largely to what might be termed movable goods rather than the larger possessions of life like real estate matters for example. This becomes very important when we have to decide the best way to serve not only our own interests but also that of others on occasions.

The Third House

The sign on the cusp and planets in this house indicate how we ought to get along with our brothers and sisters, our immediate environment and normal daily contacts like our neighbours. This might be better summed up as the way we operate our daily routines. It might also reveal how we try to influence each other in such issues. This house also governs short journeys and virtually all kinds of communication.

The Fourth House

This is mostly concerned with our domestic environment, the people in it like our parents and other near relatives. Here may be determined our attitude to buying and selling domestic property, connections with our roots, ancestors and our local and national pride, if any. Planets in this house can influence our innermost personal and private beliefs. Astrologers also look to this house for the association and effect of the mother on the subject.

The Fifth House

This shapes and moderates our attitude and preferences as to how we maintain our creativity and self-expression along with the way we enjoy the pleasures of life. Important matters like sex, pregnancy and our attitudes to children should be assessed from here. This house is also said to govern our relationships with those who are involved in our leisure moments. It can also show a love of animals, either as pets or otherwise and how we view speculation ranging from the basic light flutter to the more serious gamble.

The Sixth House

Planets here show the way in which we accept responsibilities in our employment and career. It also governs matters of service to others and how we adjust to the everyday realities of life. The Sun here often indicates our personal ambition and choice of work we do. Indeed, so would any other planet for that matter but to a lesser extent. Planets here will show how much we pay attention (or not) to detail. More personal issues like health and hygiene, diet, fitness and our personal appearance are basically influenced from this house.

These first six houses relate directly to us personally. The next six are concerned more with our attitude(s) to other people and these houses pair-off with their opposite numbers in much the same way as the signs do.

The Seventh House

This house shows partnerships and relationships, personal or otherwise. It is often called the house of marriage and, on occasions, the subject's idea of a future spouse may be detected. In essence, any planets in this house will reveal our emotional make-up. The seventh house also rules a certain amount of litigation. A survey of the planets and the ruler of the sign on the cusp should show why or with whom we are, or may be legally embroiled. This house can also show whether we have any enemies, active or otherwise.

The Eighth House

This house is traditionally associated with legacies, wills, joint monies and similar affairs. Other issues such as the possessions of those around us, their money and the end of life can also be traced. Also here may be found our attitude to big business, banks, insurance houses and stock market matters. The planet or planets in this house will also show some sexual attitudes and preferences. Planets here or the ruler of the cusp may show the level of our interest (if at all) in the mysteries of the afterlife, occultism and similar allied matters generally.

The Ninth House

This is the house to which the astrologer will look to assess our attitudes to education, religious leanings and almost all kinds of philosophy. People and places abroad as well as long distance travel and communication, foreign languages and other associated matters are connected with this house. Strongly placed planets can show a leaning toward a legal or teaching career, even the subject with which we might choose to specialise. It was not that long ago that this house was called "the house of dreams" in the sense that it dealt with our deeper, inner ambitions.

The Tenth House

Look to this house to assess our ambitions and likely career. Our reputation, personal status (always of importance to us) and our social standing within the career related area will usually be indicated by a planet or planets placed here. Our attitude to people in authority is often determined by planets in the house or by the sign on the cusp. Astrologers are also likely to look to this house for the association and effect of the father on the subject. In normal charts the cusp of this house marks the natural MC (mid-heaven) but in an Equal House map the actual point might appear in either the 9th or the 11th houses. In many cases this natural point is as important as the ascendant.

The Eleventh House

This is the house of associates rather than friends. It denotes the way we value relationships with people within any association, group or society to which we may belong. It shows the importance we place on our non-personal social life. It is from this house an astrologer will try to judge how we prefer to get along with other folk as well. It will also reveal the people with whom we have or wish to associate with because of our (or their) social position or occupation. Our humanitarian attitudes can be assessed from planets in this house.

The Twelfth House

Strictly speaking, this indicates our psychological well-being, dreams, inner fears and secret fantasies; anything likely to inhibit our self-expression. This house also reveals how and why we might withdraw to re-charge our batteries away from the gaze of the world. Our attitude to secluded places like asylums, prisons or hospitals or anything that could prove to be a source of inner worry could also be discerned from this house.

CHAPTER TWO

Looking Ahead
with the Sun

Most of us all want to do the right thing at the right time for all the right reasons, yet few of us sit down to work out a proper programme to achieve these aims. The majority of us pay only lip service to such plans and, if or when these things go wrong, blame everyone but ourselves. However, when you learn how to implement the basic principles behind astrology you can plan ahead not only to make the most of any opportunity as it occurs but also how to time and create them as well.

In the first chapter you read all about how the influence of the planets in the birth chart at the moment of your birth or any other event that is "frozen" as it is recorded in the horoscope. We are now going to learn how they appear to influence matters from a point of view.

Transits

The planets never stop travelling along their respective paths. They are constantly moving through the signs making aspects to each other and, in the case of the individual birth chart, making aspects to the natal planets and "sensitive" points in that map and their natal aspects as well. All these phenomena are known collectively as transits and are usually the easiest method of looking ahead to see what might be in store for us.

Other systems are used, such as progressions, for example, but they rely heavily on the premise of the precise accuracy of the birth data, something that cannot always be relied upon. A difference of four minutes of the birth time within a basic chart could mean predictions might be out by a year in some cases.

Transits simply compare the positions between any two or more dates however close or far apart they may be. The only problem likely to occur is with the ability of the astrologer. The interpretation of the individual planets while on the move, that is, transiting a house or a sign provides more information for us to decipher.

However, a few words of explanation concerning the interplay between houses and the signs. When you do not have your personal horoscope to refer to the signs and the houses, one can still enjoy the curious interplay found in a birth chart.

So, the first of these heavenly bodies is the Sun, normally, but not always, the most powerful influence in most horoscopes.

In order of importance the Moon comes next which, in turn, is followed by the inner planets that is Mercury, Venus and Mars.

Astrologers then turn to and assess the so-called "slow moving" bodies that are also known as the Outer Planets – Jupiter, Saturn, Uranus, Neptune and Pluto.

I have set the scene(s) for you so now all you have to is read on. Take your time – digest and enjoy at your own pace.

The Sun

While passing through Aries, Taurus, Gemini and so on, the Sun seems to exert a similar influence when it transits the houses. For example, if your Sun-sign is Aries, your "natural" second house is Taurus and your third house is Gemini. Your fourth house is Cancer and so on through to Pisces, your "natural" twelfth house. For Taurus folk advance the houses by adding one. Thus, Gemini would be the second house, Cancer, the third house and so on through to Pisces, the eleventh house, and Aries, which would be the twelfth house.

It takes a year for the Sun to travel through the zodiac and the following paragraphs show how it might affect you as it passes the different signs and houses.

The Sun in the First House

When the Sun occupies or passes through the first house it tends to give you more strength and invigorates you. You become restless, impulsive and enterprising. You feel you have to get out and about more and start new projects, explore new territory and use this new found energy as you see fit at the time. This is more or less the same as when the Sun passes through your own Sun-sign but there are a few extra indications.

Sun in Aries

So, when the Sun occupies or passes through Aries the "you" within feels a need to break free to achieve. Your personal confidence rises and you feel that it is very important to make your mark. You can become a tad selfish at any opposition, no matter how constructive it may be.

The Second House

When the Sun passes through your second house you feel the urge to acquire new possession. You might use money to enhance your personal standing in society. You are inclined to spend money on books, tools or other similar items so you that you may improve yourself or your surroundings. Businessmen often use this time to their advantage to make money on the stock market.

Sun in Taurus

There is less stress and strain and most folk seem to enjoy quieter conditions in their social and employment areas. People seem to be more diplomatic, understanding and ready to compromise.

However, some folk can become extraordinarily difficult (stubborn) or set in their ways.

The Third House

When the Sun travels through the third house the accent falls on all kinds of communication: travel, writing, teaching, talking, learning new skills and improving your immediate social life. You mix more with others, neighbours, friends and colleagues or may even take part in a local event. Short journeys are quite probable.

Sun in Gemini

People everywhere appear to be constantly on the move. All sorts of activities seem to suddenly become a focal point or points. At this time, a lot of agreements are made and deals are (or should be) signed. Partnerships will flourish if started now and life generally becomes quite busy.

The Fourth House

As the Sun moves through the fourth house, domestic matters take on an additional importance. Home life and relationships within the family circle tend to become easier all round. Older folk become more respected while the younger element is inclined to be more emotional or romantically motivated. People and or events from the past may re-enter your life.

Sun in Cancer

People tend to look for more personal security. Property dealing along with home improvements like adding a room or two or other extras can be seen almost everywhere. Traditional ways of thinking or older methods are much in evidence. National and or local politics take on more importance.

The Fifth House

The Sun in the fifth house helps improve all aspect of the social life from a simple boy-meets-girl incident to sexual encounters mostly for procreation purposes. Children tend to play a larger role on the life possibly in the recreational or sporting worlds. The individual; tends to put him or herself before others because there is a need to better oneself no matter how it may be achieved. Gambling, for a small flutter to an out-and-out large-scale wager is likely.

Sun in Leo

This is like play time for many – people tend to enjoy sport of all kinds while the theatre and the entertainment world are likely to enjoy a new lease of life. People tend to cycle more and travel under their own steam where they can. Rambling, boating, hiking or hill-climbing are also possible. Great plans are conceived but not a lot goes much further than that when it comes to actually doing anything along these lines.

The Sixth House

As the Sun travels through the sixth house it triggers off everything and anything to do with the working arena together with all the responsibilities that goes with it. The Sun here also affects anything to do with health for good or ill. Diet regimes of all kinds attract and keeping fit and maintaining all is well takes on added importance, perhaps more for the younger element than the older folk. For some, entertainment matters could come more to the fore as people turn to the creative arts.

Sun in Virgo

Things seem to slow down and people stop and think more before taking any action. They want to attend to details more than usual.

While some folk look to their employment conditions others may go back to the classroom. Evening school or other paces or systems of learning flourish. Virgo is a practical sign and those who are clever with their hands feel they must become more involved to maintain their skills.

The Seventh House

The Sun really does shine here and tends to enhance all manner of relationships and partnerships because people matter. These issues may be just ordinary friendships or the more serious affairs like marriage and beyond (?). The desire to be noticed is always strong at this time and many go to extreme lengths to ensure that they are noticed by those who matter. How you handle public relations and your legal obligations may well surface.

Sun in Libra

Everybody seems to want to get along with everybody one way or another. However, a few underhand deals are likely about now, so this is the time to remember that what you see is not always what you get. Money or associated matters may be a problem, especially in the middle of the period. This is not a god time to go-it-alone; you should work with other folk for the best results. Many people tend to plan their winter holiday about now.

The Eighth House

When traversing this house the Sun helps to increase your sex drive. Financial issues are brought to your attention especially joint resources, taxes or inheritance matters. It is about now that many people consider to or actually do make out their last will and testament. There may well be some concern for the welfare of your children whatever their age. Often, the music business helps to create opportunity for those who really try.

27

Sun in Scorpio

Life tends to get a little more serious as people become suddenly concerned with many of the more important issues of life. Feelings tend to be much of a do-or-die affair. Attitudes may firm up as many folk stand up for what they feel is their right. People seem to love or hate with equal intensity. Investigative activities, manufacturing and the creative industries flourish.

The Ninth House

When the Sun passes through this house all kinds of personal educational matters take on an extra importance. A new series of studies may begin furnishing you with a knowledge you may have always wanted. Long-distance communications, affairs abroad or a first journey overseas become possible. Some issues need to be personally instigated or you may be caught up in the plans of other folk. People of business matters from overseas may enter your life.

Sun in Sagittarius

This is a dual natured sign and it depends on the age of the individual as to how he or she will experience this period. The younger folk may get out of hand and lack discipline and a sense of responsibility. Older people are inclined to spend their leisure time in more competitive activities. Anything that needs attention to detail must be dealt with carefully.

The Tenth House

As the Sun passes through the tenth house, your personal status and all your ambitions are highlighted. Your career and place in society, your personal standing, local level, political aspirations and contacts with people (especially those in authority) all come under this influence. Any past indiscretions you have tried to keep quiet could surface now. If this is so – just think of the possible damage this might cause.

Sun in Capricorn

People tend to want to better just about everything they have – a bigger and better car, house, job and status at work. The general idea is making and take those extra steps as you start to grow older. Nearly all relationship are likely to suffer as you try to create what you think is a better life for you and yours. Organised life attracts quite strongly.

The Eleventh House

Here, the Sun influences the way you think you ought to fit into society. People tend to review their part in all manner of relationships and try to better themselves where they feel it to be necessary to do so. Many folk see themselves as one of if not the leader in their community life. Some may stand in elections in whatever group to which they belong. They want to be the head, the director, chairman or even the mayor if in local politics.

Sun in Aquarius

Personal appearance becomes rather more important about now. While some may relax and follow the current mode, there are some who will try to lead. Older folk start to dress down while the younger element tend to smarten up. Generally speaking the atmosphere is rather easy-going because most people tend to get along quite well with each other. Future long-term plans may be discussed and laid about now.

The Twelfth House

As the Sun passes through this house many secret matters become known. Hitherto liaisons that ought never to become public knowledge somehow come to light. Old habits and beliefs come under scrutiny. It becomes evident that changes need to be made for this is the end of a twelve-month period so cut out deadwood. Forget what cannot (or should not) be continued and make ready for a fresh start – if possible. Some may start to pursue occult or mysterious beliefs and or practices.

Sun in Pisces

Almost anything can and is likely to happen during the Sun's transit of this house. People can be a bit "stiff" one moment and quite cheerful the next. Most folk tend to be a tad susceptible to all sorts of influences, perhaps a little too impressionable at times. Health matters may worry a few folk. Diet consciousness and keep-fit regimes can attract – but rarely for too long.

These guidelines of what to expect when the Sun travels through the heavens are conditioned by the current positions of the other planets and their possible aspects not only to each other but also to the Sun and other natal planets or parts of the horoscope.

To get used to these ideas simply reflect on where the Sun was when you said or did this or that at the time. More importantly – look ahead for this might help you to look at matters in a different light giving you an opportunity to take advantage accordingly.

CHAPTER THREE

Looking Ahead with the Moon

The Moon is the fastest moving of the heavenly bodies and takes about a month to pass through the individual signs at the speed of about one sign every other day on average. As a rule, she travels at slightly different speeds which can vary from week to week and month to month.

She rules the instinctual side of our nature, our moods or unconscious responses to our daily life. She reflects an influence or power rather than instigating situations because she has no light of her own. She is all things to all men – literally.

When aspected by the Sun she will reflect its influence. When she is in aspect with Mercury, or any other planet for that matter, she adopts and takes on that planet's effect regulated by where she and the other planet may be. A lot also depends on what part of her phase she is in.

Lunar Phases

At the time of a New Moon, she is conjunct, or in the same place as the Sun. It is the start of her waxing phase in the First Quarter. The Second Quarter occurs when she is in a square aspect with the Sun, or halfway toward the Full Moon when she is in opposition aspect to the Sun. At this, the start of the Third Quarter, her waning phase begins and as her power weakens, she is said to be disseminating to the Last Quarter where she is once again in square aspect to the Sun.

An astrologer can often tell in which phase an individual was born by the way a person tends to act. If born at the New Moon, the personality is rather bubbly and full of tremendous enthusiasm for anything that takes their fancy at the time. However, this type tends to be rather subjective and, if they do not put themselves first, they will certainly be near the forefront in all their undertakings. They really are very impulsive folk.

People born at the First Quarter are active, have very positive views and do not take very kindly to any opposition, however well meant. Often, they are inclined to innovate, change, or introduce fresh methods of doing things. There is often a stubborn streak that is evident once these people get the bit between their teeth.

Those born at the Full Moon have the gift of being able to see both sides of a question but the prevailing mood of the moment often influences their decision. Quite creative in their own way, they have a certain logic that defies description at times. But, despite this they always have engaging personalities.

Those born at the Last Quarter often become involved more with people than things. They have a gift for understanding the frailties of their fellow beings and they excel at counselling and guidance work. There is a natural talent for mediation but, curiously, they are often are often difficult to understand or get to know intimately.

The Moon's position will be found in an ephemeris along with all the other planetary bodies but, because of her speed, it is not possible to list anything here but these are guidelines of how she may influence you as she transits the different signs and houses.

The Moon in the First House

As the Moon travels through your first house you will be eager to start new ventures, to get things going. You won't want to sit around waiting for things to happen; you want to make them happen. Avoid all impulsive behaviour. Stop – think – then act.

Moon in Aries

Inclined to be rather bossy and order others around. Set up new projects with caution, enlist in the armed services or join a sports club. Take things one stage at a time and try not to scatter your energies. If mistakes are made now, they could prove to be quite costly in the long run.

The Second House

Money matters matter. There is a tendency to be extravagant and waste cash; to buy things for the sake of buying. This favours the ladies and their interests mostly. Material security or the lack of it can occupy the individual. Buy things for the home, food, furnishings etc.

Moon in Taurus

This is a splendid time to entertain people. Buy or sell property, take up a new job in a service industry or open a bank account. It is also a good time to propose marriage and get engaged. People tend to be cautious or practical at this time and new ideas are not always well received.

The Third House

The Moon here favours immediate family matters, business communications and catching up on correspondence. Short journey are either necessary or become that way. Buy or sell books, make time for those cosy little chats but don't give away all your secrets. Try something new.

Moon in Gemini

Make phone calls, write letters and pay bills. It pays to be adaptable, to talk and listen, and to let others make the running.

Moods can change very quickly and some people are liable to be two-faced. It is best to rely on your sixth sense rather than the facts.

The Fourth House

Relationships or the welfare of parents or other elderly family members need to be worked on. People or events from the past re-enter the life. Some folk prove to be quite narrow-minded and traditional thinking predominates when modern matters are discussed.

Moon in Cancer

Child welfare and their concerns are important. People may be defensive or over-sensitive to criticism. Over indulgence or a lack of exercise can affect physical well-being. There is a tendency to gloss over past glories or hold on to memories for too long.

The Fifth House

Emotional matters associated with sex and procreation becomes highlighted. Many people are inclined to gambling of all kinds. The need to take a chance is strong. Attend a sports gathering, visit the theatre or go to a cinema. Throw or go to a party.

Moon in Leo

People can be over-bearing or try to take charge, especially at work. Favouritism is rife and some folk may try to take advantage or seize the advantage for themselves. Good personal appearance helps steal the limelight so that you are noticed by those have influence.

The Sixth House

Have a health check-up, attend to diet and hygiene, have a spring-clean no matter what the season, clean up around the house, have a make-over, improve your employment/career chances. May over-do attention to detail and can be over-fussy.

Moon in Virgo

This transit favours practical artistic creation, design work, music or even sculpting. In the kitchen and make bread or wine. Prepare dishes for eating at a later date. Prepare a business presentation and be ready to take advantage as opportunity presents itself.

The Seventh House

Mostly, all forms of partnerships and relationships are high-lighted. Be accessible and ready to co-operate. Compromise, use diplomacy, make joint decisions; do not go it alone. Try to remember, that any conflict which does arise will be emotionally orientated.

Moon in Libra

Get out and about, have a shopping spree with a friend, buy perfume, new clothes, wedding wear or jewellery. Indulge yourself – have a sauna. If there is a problem, avoid sitting on the fence but do support one side or the other.

The Eighth House

Check private documentation, insurance policies, taxes and licences. Pay bills before a red demand arrives. All private or personal matters should be kept that way, play your cards close to your chest and play a lone hand. Watch your temper.

Moon in Scorpio

Maintain personal dignity – avoid dishing the dirt. Try also to avoid visiting hospitals or having surgical operations. Do not go shopping for clothes or try on new shoes. Good for agriculture and the farming business. Investigative work is also favoured and making discreet enquiries or operating in behind the scenes activities.

The Ninth House

People are outspoken, direct and to the point. Educational, legal and religious matters, especially for women, may be highlighted. There is often an accent on travel matters. Family journeys, long distance for pleasure or business purposes. This can be a restless period.

Moon in Sagittarius

Sporting activities, athletics, horse or motor, air or sea racing competitions may be pursued. Rambling, mountain climbing – being different is really the key factor. People have a need to shake off the cobwebs and acting differently like this helps.

The Tenth House

Protect your personal status, especially at work. Ambitions and career moves may all need extra effort. Deal with the boss, not a minion and that way you get noticed. Set up new schemes, start your own business. Push for what you think is rightfully yours and don't let up until it is. This can be a short but serious period.

Moon in Capricorn

This could be a practical period in every sense of the word. Get things done and ensure that others are making progress with their designated tasks. Be the boss and make decisions. Avoid emotional considerations, but try not to be too inflexible.

The Eleventh House

Enjoy all forms of group social activities. Promote a community spirit. Adopt a broad-minded attitude – you may have to. If you deal with the younger element be prepared to show your humanitarian side. Act on an impulse and surprise loved ones. Try to get to church.

Moon in Aquarius

Domestic and family relationships with people outside this circle will come to the forefront. Go shopping for electronic goods, computers and hi-fi or similar. Repair gas, electric or water pipes; install a new phone line. Experiment, eat out somewhere new.

The Twelfth House

Everyone needs to keep their feet on the ground and be as realistic as they can. People can be moody, unpredictable and a tad more sensitive than may be usual. What you see is not always what you get and a degree of deviousness is always apparent with the Moon in this position.

Moon in Pisces

There may be a tendency to overdo or over-indulge in the pleasures of life – drink, drugs and/or sex. Emotions can run riot at the drop of the hat and people seem to view the world through rose coloured glasses. On a more mundane level, fill the car, have a pedicure. Fall in or make love.

These Lunar guidelines in respect of the way she spends time in each of the houses and signs are not set in tablets of stone. Much will depend on your particular mood of the moment and whether or not you feel it might be worth the effort to make the effort as suggested.

The Moon has often been accused of being a fickle lady and what is recommended here might well require a little more study before you decide on what you are going to do, if indeed, you feel that there is something you have (or ought) to do.

CHAPTER FOUR

Looking Ahead with the Inner Planets

Mercury, Venus and Mars

These three planets are the inner, fast moving heavenly bodies and the first we meet that can also appear to travel backwards at certain times of the year. This is called retrograde motion. The Sun and Moon never actually move, or seem to move, backward at any time. But, because of certain astronomical phenomena, some planets sometimes do appear to travel in reverse.

All the heavenly bodies travel around the Sun from west to east in what is commonly termed direct motion. Because of the earth's own speed circumstances arise where the planets appear to slow down and look as though they may have actually stopped. This short spell is called a "station"; in this particular case, stationary retrograde for, after a short while the planet will start moving again – but in reverse direction, or retrograde motion.

At the end of the retrograde period, the planet again appears to slow down and then seem to stop. This is the "stationary direct" mode and, following another short spell the planet begins to move once again – in direct motion.

Astrologers differ as to how retrograde planets should be interpreted. Some of them ignore the phenomenon altogether while others take serious note. However, it is generally accepted and agreed that when a planet is at a station prior to moving one way or another the influence it exerts is very strong and must be taken into account.

In many cases when a planet is at a station, it can and does usurp the power of the ruling and or ascending planet. Mostly, interpretation is left to the discretion of the astrologer although that all depends on the school of thought that he or she belongs. These days more and more of those new to the study now take retrograde more seriously.

Mercury

Mercury, the nearest planet to the Sun, travels around it in about 88 days on average. It is responsible for how we communicate with others. It rules how we speak to people, depending on our relative status, how we think and interpret information coming in or going out. The way we speak, the tone we adopt and the speech patterns we generally employ are also governed by Mercury. It also has sway over the way we actually write to other people and even how we walk.

Mercury governs the five senses and has an effect on the sixth as well. Mercury warns of the good or the bad. He is the arbiter of our taste. He indicates what we should feel and, when it comes to smell, he guides us accordingly. This is most helpful when it comes to the multitude of aromas in our everyday surroundings that are liable to turn us off or on.

Mercury rules all we hear and the way we interpret these sounds. With certain people, some noises may be positively loathed while others adore them. Just think of the appreciation and interpretation of music that can and does vary so much between people who are close in so many other different ways yet differ so widely in their audio tastes.

Lastly, there is our sight. What we see, and how it can move us in one mood or direction comes under the jurisdiction of the little planet whose name in another ancient language meant the Messenger of the Gods. Along with all of these external methods of communication, Mercury has other responsibilities, for he also rules our internal communications system.

He rules the way the five senses allow, persuade or react and cause you to take certain physical actions dependent on the message(s) received. He allows for the collaboration of mind and hand, ear, eye, memories and a thousand different things every hour of every day.

He constantly helps you to remember all types of information, and then stores the data in your memory banks ready for retrieval later. Mercury is a very important influence in your life – none more so when he makes a transit over the important places and planets of your natal chart. When he turns retrograde, the period that he is stationary is important and it accentuates his influence accordingly. While retrograde, as a rule for about 24 days, you have time to re-think strategy; you have time to re-evaluate what has happened before and make changes where necessary.

When he becomes stationary just before he turns direct again, he goads you into one more review and then proceeds to implement your plans and ideas as you may now see fit.

The relationship between the Moon and Mercury is very important. If the Moon was travelling fast at your birth and Mercury was in direct motion your natural perception rate should be high. If the Moon was slow and (or) Mercury was retrograde, you might have trouble understanding matters when they are first presented to you.

Mercury in Transit

As Mercury in transit moves over any sensitive part in your chart or is stationary or retrograde, how you receive and understand information and take whatever action is deemed necessary can and will be affected. However, because of the speed with which Mercury travels, these matters are more of a daily nature but they may account for why some days are an absolute breeze and you cope well while other times, quite frankly, are best forgotten.

As a rule, about three times a year or so, Mercury goes retrograde and while it is so, all manner of things are likely to go wrong with communication(s) of all kinds. The post can be delayed, promised phone calls are not made or returned, cheques or other payments fail to arrive and you are unable to get new projects off the ground. People experience travel problems where they least expect them. In all probability your computer develops a fault or the Internet packs up. The best thing to do is finish all outstanding tasks but start nothing new.

Your memory becomes faulty so review what you want to do, for you are likely to find errors where you least expect them.

The daily motion and positions of Mercury are recorded in an ephemeris and are well worth noting when important matters are on the horizon. If Mercury is favourable, let the good times roll; but if his position is adverse, take remedial action and prepare properly for the event.

Venus

Venus is the second planet from the Sun and, on average, orbits it in about 225 days. She decides how we evaluate our life from an emotional point of view. She also governs with whom and how we love or share our affections. If we are in a hateful mood it is Venus who decides how far we go. If we feel we want to indulge ourselves she will also set those parameters.

When we feel all soft and warm, or are pleased with the outcome of a particular event, it is Venus who decides the level of self-indulgence for she governs the nice things as well as measuring our negative moments. The quality and quantity of all these self-indulgent moments, no matter what they are, are all under her domain.

When you have that sudden urge to buy a drink or a bag of sweets, a bar of chocolate, or that very special brand of cigarettes or have the urge to go on a proper buying spree for clothes or shoes, perfume or jewellery, it will probably be as a result of Venus transiting a rather sensitive part in your natal chart.

This planet not only also influences the way we spend money, she also holds sway over what we want for permanent or temporary possessions and that includes our personal appearance and style, such as jewellery and other items of adornment. For example, until only recently only men were associated with tattoos but it is now the current vogue for ladies of all ages to have delicate little pictures placed in rather personal positions, a typical ploy of Venus in the battle of the sexes.

Women with Venus in Libra almost always show exquisite taste when it comes to personal appearance and especially with jewellery. Men with Venus in Aquarius tend to favour the one heavy ring in the ear. With both, gold is probably more favoured than silver while people of either sex with Venus in Cancer tend to prefer silver.

Venus in Transit

Every eighteen months or so, Venus turns retrograde for about six weeks – it depends on varying astronomical factors. When she goes stationary retrograde people become extra sensitive emotionally. As a rule, partnerships and relationships tend to suffer one way or another because moods swings can and do get out of hand. But, despite the speed with which Venus moves, means these moods will be simply transient affairs and not last too long. They can wreak havoc in any relationship, however personal or impersonal it may be. Money matters really do matter. What is said and done at such times is best forgotten, if possible.

As a rule, these moods are liable to bring an intensity of purpose, or a lazy streak can take over. People sacrifice their spare time to help but the less fortunate; they become martyrs for a cause. Some suddenly doubt the sincerity of friends or workplace colleagues. They may even try to investigate to see if they are right or not. It is a hazardous period if you say or do the wrong thing if someone is affected in this way.

When Venus transits Taurus money is well spent but when she passes through Virgo, the accent is on practicality. Capricorn has a sense of both taste and practicality. All three are Earth signs, so, when in the Fire signs Venus will accentuate the self but while in Air signs it suggests the intellect will be reflected in their purchases. Venus in a Water sign always allows the emotions full sway. If the mood is right, then there will be few problems. But, when the mood is wrong, people can be demon shoppers.

The daily motion and positions of Venus are recorded in an ephemeris and are always worth noting if you want things to proceed smoothly. When Venus is favourable then, as with Mercury, let the good times roll. But if she is adverse, be ready to cast oil upon the waters.

Mars

Mars, the fourth planet from the Sun, takes on average about 22 months or so to travel around it (the Earth is the third planet, remember). The Red Planet is also the first real symbol of action, aggression and self-assertion in our exploration of the planets of the zodiac.

When Mars is in full sway, it is a "Me first – women and children next" situation all the time and every time. Mars means anger, controlled or spontaneous; he has rule over your passions whether you direct it or when you act on impulse. All your bravery, how you face up to others, or the way you fight for what you feel is rightfully yours is under the domain of the Red Planet.

He governs the spirit of adventure, determines your fight plan and gets you all fired up. He will make you act passionately but not necessarily positively. He is also destructive. Curiously, he also makes you regret what you may have said or done to achieve your aim for, while he determines your headstrong actions, he doesn't count the cost of having to pay for the damage or retribution from other sources. He is dangerous; therefore, not only to others, but also to yourself for there is no concern with safety factors at all. Unfortunately, you often only find this out when it is too late – the damage has been done.

Mars in Transit

In the first house Mars makes you wilful and not content to stand by and watch because he has to take an active part. When in your second house, Mars insists that the way you earn your money has to have some element of danger associated with it. Thus, it can be seen that when in each of the houses Mars must have an element of action, aggression and assertiveness in whatever the house represents.

Mars turns retrograde about every two years for up to 70 days in some cases during which time his influence becomes more important than usual. He also tends to remain stationary for slightly longer than is usual and, at some time during this period, Mars is opposite the Sun by aspect. When Mars is in this position people's personalities change radically, the drive and enthusiasm that you normally associate with them suddenly appears to be lacking.

When there is less conflict, no open aggression; it is almost as if someone somewhere had pressed a button and the lights went out. The character becomes more amenable, he or she can be dealt with in a far more civil atmosphere and in a less challenging manner. The whole personality can change quite radically which can be seen by the way the person concerned makes the effort to control their normal enthusiasm, the way they take care not to offend.

Some folk are unable to fulfil their normal obligations while Mars is retrograde. Men may go off sex or lose their drive for a while and the ladies may make less effort in their appearance and demeanour. Either sex who especially like sport tend to involve themselves from a spectator's point of view while some choose to work behind the scenes.

No matter which house Mars is in when it is retrograde, there will be a radical change of heart associated with the meaning of that house. So, in the fourth house, for example, someone who does not normally get on with his family will do so and so on.

Just before he turns direct again, Mars imprints his influence on the chart in no uncertain times. It is like a racing driver revving through the gears prior to releasing the brake. Once that brake is released, so are all the energies that have been pent up. You will certainly know it when it happens to you personally or someone near you.

The daily motion and positions of Mars are recorded in an ephemeris and should be kept under observation at all times. With Mars, timing is an art. It is always worth keeping an eye open if you prefer the peaceful life and like things to go smoothly.

CHAPTER FIVE

Looking Ahead with the Outer Planets

Jupiter, Saturn, Uranus, Neptune and Pluto

When each of these five slow-moving outer planets decide it is time to wield their powerful influences in your natal chart, or by transit, you soon get to know about it. Individually, they exert enormous power dependent on their position in the chart but, if they should combine by aspect, then their collective influence will cause you to make radical changes often without notice or a warning of intent.

One moment, you may be quietly getting along with your life, the next, you find yourself in the middle of a period of change often with long term and far-reaching consequences.

It is rare for these changes to be all good or all bad but, generally speaking, it can be said that Jupiter, Uranus and Neptune are largely beneficial but Saturn and Pluto are considered troublesome. Now, while this is mainly true, these planets frequently introduce what seems to be a hard time but only for you to find later that it was all for the best in the long run. And because they move so very slowly, any influence they do exert can last a long time, months or even years in some cases.

Jupiter

Known affectionately as the "greater benefic" this planet takes about 11.86 years to travel around the Sun staying in one sign for about a year or so, depending on certain astronomical circumstances. As Jupiter transits a house or a sign, it increases the social niceties associated with it. Cultural matters and your personal self-expression become easier. Your popularity increases, you are able to expand your interests in all of these areas.

While in a house or sign, affairs to do with that house or sign seem to flow along quite easily. As a rule, what you usually set out to achieve is successful. Jupiter is primarily concerned with education, religion and the law as well as people in power, officialdom and other positions of influence like the boss, your teacher or a member of the police force.

When Jupiter turns retrograde, for around 120 days on average, people become more self-interested. Their eye is always on the main chance for them to benefit as various opportunities are presented. Such folk usually manage to benefit through very careful planning – itself a fine art at the best of times.

For example, when retrograde Jupiter transits the fifth house or is in Leo, people's emotional lives may be in turmoil. Yet these folk manage to turn it all to their advantage and pass on to another relationship where they construct a new association that not only benefits their new partner but themselves as well.

When retrograde Jupiter passes through the twelfth house people spend much of their free time helping the less fortunate and, while doing so, learn a lot more about themselves. Some even take up such work as part of a new career change.

Saturn

This planet is the symbol of responsibility, conservatism, discipline and construction. It takes about 29.46 years to travel around the Sun and around two and a half years or so to transit a house or a sign. It is the great limiter. When Saturn transits a house or a sign your sense of responsibility in matters associated with it develop. You quickly learn how to shoulder problems and deal with them – properly or else!

Saturn transiting one of the water signs can make people's emotions become too strong for them to handle correctly and some feel vulnerable or are unable to cope with their fears. As it travels through the fire signs it makes individuals experience a lack of confidence. They may lack a sense of purpose and many become quite selfish or too proud to seek help when they need it the most.

In the air signs, Saturn influences the way a person communicates their innermost thoughts. There may be a lack of trust even with a very close partner and they may suffer from feelings of inadequacy. When passing through the earth signs, Saturn will make a person worry unnecessarily about his or her possessions, material things, their comforts and personal security.

When Saturn turns retrograde, in some cases for up to four to five months at a time, these affairs can take on an added mystery or make the individual unable to see things clearly or in their proper perspective. It is rather like the fate line in palmistry. If you have one, then you feel limited by it. Yet, when you look beyond the boundaries you create for yourself, you see that they can easily be transcended if you plan properly. Some say that a retrograde Saturn can (on occasions) influence the individual or events rather in a not too dissimilar fashion like a direct motion Jupiter.

Uranus

This is the first of the more recently discovered planets in our system and takes about 84.02 years to travel around the Sun sometimes staying in one sign for up to seven or more years depending on the prevailing astronomical circumstances. It is the planet of change. Uranus (pronounced "yur-an-us") breaks with tradition, the tried and trusted. It makes us find new ways of doing things and creates lateral thinking as it does so. It is the sign of the rebel, the anarchist or the nihilist. It really means no harm and from the changes it brings almost always comes good.

All those unexpected circumstances and events, your involvement in society generally, modern technology like computers and the Internet are ruled by Uranus as it travels slowly around the solar system. As it passes through each house and sign, it makes you break with old ideas and introduces new ways – and they are always sudden affairs. Occasionally, you may have an inkling of what to expect in the back of your mind but, as a rule, change comes about very swiftly indeed.

For example, when Uranus passes through the first house or Aries, you begin to experience a change of attitude to almost everything. You may suffer from inner tension and your actions become unpredictable. There will be changes and, sometimes, they are so radical you undergo a total transformation in all you do or believe in.

As this planet turns retrograde – for up to 150 days at times – it tends to unsettle people and they become quite difficult to get along with, perhaps because they want to make changes to established routine or to reform or dig for the (possible) hidden motives as to why people act or believe in things the way they do.

Neptune

The planet of dreams and ideals takes 164.79 years to travel around the Sun and can sometimes stay in one sign for up to fourteen years. Mostly, its influence is regarded in a generation sense or theme. So many people have Neptune in the same house or sign that one can discern an overall perception of the way they all seem to reflect similar tendencies in the affairs of the house or sign concerned.

For example, most people born between late 1920 and 1943 have Neptune in Virgo display idealism in one way or another with health and diet, cleanliness, occupation and working conditions. Those born between 1943 and 1956 have Neptune in Libra and are rather too idealistic about close emotional partnerships. The separation and divorce rate of their marriages will bear this out.

As Neptune passes through a house or sign it stirs up the emotions and the imagination. The issues concerned may well become clouded, escapist tendencies come about. Some may turn to religion or have psychic experiences. Inspiration and intuition blend well in those who are involved in any of the artistic and creative fields.

When Neptune turns retrograde, perhaps for up to 159 days at a time, people become evasive, vague and try to bluff their way through life. There is a tendency to refuse to commit themselves to a clearly defined course of action regarding the affairs of the house or sign concerned. There seems to be a lack of self-confidence and they appear as idle dreamers, or just plain confused.

Often, they are left to their own devices by others but what they need is to be taken under the wing of someone stronger who can cope and direct their lives in a better way. However, occasionally, some can be extremely creative.

Pluto

Strictly speaking, Pluto is no longer accepted as a planet and has been recently downgraded. However, its influence is still strong in a chart and most astrologers still use it. This is the last of the outer planets to have been discovered – so far. It takes about 248.4 years to journey around the Sun and its stay in a house or sign can last thirty years in some cases or only fifteen years in others because of its highly individualistic and erratic orbit.

By sign, Pluto is a planet that influences generations. Pluto opens up all of our innermost fears and releases them to be publicly dissected, to be eliminated and transformed. But Pluto also means power. Wherever it is in a house or sign there will be an intensity of purpose. When In the first house, it make us impose our will to get things done; in the second, it creates an obsession for material gain and acquisition, while in the seventh house there is a constant struggle for power and supremacy in any kind of relationship, and so on through the houses and signs.

Before it can properly build anything it has first to destroy what is presently there. The most constantly used word is regeneration or the death of the old ways, then the initiation of the new changes. Pluto, because of its very slow movement can be found in any house of the natal birth chart and exerts the more influence there. The sign it is in is of lesser significance.

As it turns retrograde for up to 160 days or so, Pluto tends to create tremendous concentration, a single-mindedness of energy and purpose to attain and achieve. When in this mode people can appear to be quite rude. It is like having two simian lines as in palmistry. People seem to have few, if any, inhibitions, just the will to attain, achieve and succeed as if there are no limits to have to avoid.

CHAPTER SIX

Looking Ahead with an Explanation of Transits

Retrograde Motion
Planets Fast or Slow
Planets OOB

When you are working with one individual, the first step is to prepare his or her natal chart and compare the planetary positions for the date in question to those in the horoscope.

Each of the transiting planetary positions and their aspects to all of the natal planets and their aspects must be assessed. As a rule, their effects are not necessarily limited to that place, but are what might be called a compound affair. There are a number of other matters that must also be taken into account.

For example, transiting Jupiter could be making a favourable aspect to natal Venus while Pluto could be creating an unstable situation with a negative aspect to natal Mars or Uranus that detracts from the benefit of the Jupiter/Venus contact.

Alternatively, if transiting Neptune were stationary retrograde on natal Saturn's position with transiting Sun conjunct natal

Moon, the negative effect of the former aspect would be most unhelpful. All these points are very important and must be remembered as a chart is assessed.

We have not yet mentioned asteroids, comets, fixed stars, eclipses and midpoints, none of which have a place for discussion here other than to say that it would be rare for an astrologer to take *all* of these extra features into account. Nevertheless, they are there and should be considered.

However, this simply is not a practical or workable exercise. There are also at least 150 fixed stars to be consulted, five principle asteroids along with a host of minor ones. A solar, lunar, or a partial or total eclipse could exert its effect and, in some cases, even a comet might have to be considered.

Then there are the midpoints, the middle distance between the planetary aspects, their positions and their orbs. In essence, a descent into an almost total madness from which most astrologers normally refrain.

Strictly speaking, they should include all this extra data but practise and plain old-fashioned common sense imply otherwise. Cynics might say that if astrologers were to consult all of this material then whatever the advice they could couch it all in less nebulous terms. After all, once all the facts have been taken into account, the end result would have to be much more to the point!

Quite right too, but it just isn't practical.

More and more these days, because of the doubt about the accuracy of a birth time which is not always recorded properly in this country – nor is the actual date in quite a few cases In these cases it is much easier to measure and assess relationships and events in the simplest way possible.

The outer planets, Jupiter, Saturn, Uranus, Neptune and Pluto decide it is time to wield their individual influences in your natal chart, or by transit, you soon get know about it!

Individually, they exert enormous power dependent on their position in the chart but, if they should combine by aspect then their collective influence will cause you to make radical changes ofen without notice or warning of intent.

One moment you may be getting along with your life, the next, you find yourself in the middle of a period of change often with long term and far-reaching consequences.

It is rare for these changes to be all good or all bad but, generally speaking, it can be said that Jupiter, Uranus and Neptune are largely beneficial but Saturn and Pluto are considered to be troublesome. Now while this is mainly true, these planets frequently introduce what seems to be a hard time but only for you to find later that it was all for the best in the long run. And because they move so very slowly, the influences they do exert can last a long time, months or even years in some cases.

So, the transiting inner planets are employed to record daily or weekly forecasts with, occasionally, the inclusion of an aspect or position of one of the slower moving outer planets thrown in to add to the weight of what might be expected.

In this series of twelve forecasts I deal with each zodiac sign in some depth. I have examined each of the outer planets to assess their effect that they should exert as they orbit each of the signs from 1 January 2021 until 31 December 2130.

As you read what to expect for yourself, or for those who are close to you, think of how you may best time matters to make the most of all the opportunities. But also remember to hold back when things may seem to be adverse.

It is all a question of choosing the right time. That is what astrology is all about – timing.

Retrograde Motion

Every so often each of the planets with the exception of the Sun and the Moon appear to stop, stay put for a short period and then begin to (apparently) move backwards. This is called retrograde motion and, while it certainly appears to be travelling backwards the planet concerned does not actually move in this direction at all. It only seems like it when the heavenly bodies are viewed from the Earth at such times.

Some astrologers tend to ignore this procedure altogether while others just make a few notes. Quite a few, however, feel that this is very important and always look to see if there are any planets in retrograde motion for they say this extremely important when creating a chart or looking at transits.

When you look in an ephemeris for either your birth data or for planetary transits you will see the word "STAT" or the initials "SD" or "SR". The word means the planet concerned is apparently "stationary" prior to moving either forward or "stationary" before it turns retrograde.

Once again there are distinct schools of thought. Some feel this position accentuates the power of the planet while others tend to ignore it altogether. Logically, if a planet is (apparently) standing still irrespective of which way it may appear to be travelling then in such circumstances the sign and the house that such a planet occupies at the time must take on an added importance.

For those readers who have their own chart or who are looking at transits should find the following comments on planets that are stationary or retrograde helpful as they assess a birth chart.

Mercury

When this planet is in retrograde motion in a birth chart there is a tendency for the subject to be shy, slightly reserved and seemingly "slow" on the uptake. They may often have problems in putting their ideas over to others. These people need a little more time than usual to mull things over; to assess a situation before they make their move. They are not dull or thick as some might think. In fact, they are very often quite the opposite.

This planet turns retrograde up to three or four times a year at four month intervals for periods of about 24 days. As it moves from one direction to the other it seems to stop and this is called a stationary position. If Mercury is stationary retrograde it suggests an emphasis depending on the house and or sign in which it found.

Venus

When this planet is retrograde in the birth chart there is often a love of love of money and possessions for these people are rarely at a loss or poor – they are too security minded. Many become involved in unusual emotional relationships either with a definite age difference or a seeming "mismatch" of the pair. There could be a lack of femininity in a woman while a man could be more of a gentle soul than most – but neither is necessarily homosexual. There is often a definite creative or artistic streak in the nature.

Venus moves retrograde for up to 40 days at a time at approximately 18 month intervals. When in a stationary position it accentuates the meaning of the house or sign in which it is found. The subject may be less fussy about their personal comfort and more easily pleased with things in general. Sport and business matters attract and these subjects seem to have a natural affinity for such things.

Mars

When Mars is retrograde the subject may appear lazy and uncommitted but nothing could be further from the truth. These people should never be under-estimated, for they will know just how and when to act – their timing is often very good. Indeed, there is a gift for doing things at the right moment – and win. However, there is almost always some difficulty in expressing their emotions clearly.

When Mars moves stationary retrograde it often stays in the same position for up to seven or more days every two years or so. It can remain retrograde for up to 70 days. When in a stationary position it tends to accentuate the meaning of the house and sign in which it is found but in general terms any "sting" in the nature of the subject becomes less obvious. If he or she is going to oppose a person or an event, they will do it from the side lines and you won't know much about it until the deed is done.

Jupiter

When this planet is retrograde, the subject is likely to be a lot more patient than average. He or she is mostly clever but they can also be quite idealistic at the expense of practicality. Sport attracts but not so much as a player but, perhaps, more in one of the roles behind the team or teams. They make very good trainers and do a lot of good as a referee or an umpire. They often seem to be modest but this is far from the truth for if they have to they will re-write rules to suit themselves.

Jupiter turns retrograde once every year and usually stays that way for about 120 days or so but when it is stationary it accentuates the house or sign in which it appears and can act rather like having a second Saturn in their chart. This can hold them back until they are absolutely sure of their ground before they proceed. Thus they can act at times like barrack-room lawyers nosing here, there and everywhere until they are satisfied of the facts as they see them.

Saturn

When this planet is retrograde in the chart the subject will display an air of either over-cautiousness or over-expansiveness in their overall attitude, as if there are no half measures. They experience self-doubt along with a seeming lack of self-confidence. Often they want to turn the clock back and have another attempt at a project that did not quite go the way they wanted or expected. Saturn like this acts a lot like Jupiter in forward motion. So, when they feel expansive they throw everything to the winds and act like there is no tomorrow. This planet usually turns retrograde for anything up to 140 days at a time once a year.

Uranus

Uranus retrograde in any chart usually creates a fairly strong inclination toward being impractical. In their own eyes the subjects are never wrong and can appear dreadfully dogmatic. He or she is a born rebel, someone who is constantly wanting or trying to reform everything and everyone. This is a sure sign of a changeable personality, one who will often move house or change course at the slightest whim. People from both sexes are often very interested in astrology and or other related subjects in a practical sense. When Uranus moves retrograde once a year, it does so for around 150 days at a time once a year but does not move very far at such times.

Neptune

When this planet is retrograde and especially when it is stationary it gives the subject a far better grip on practicality and reality. These subjects may well be very intuitive and may appear to be quite psychic in some cases. These people are best left to use their talents in such a way that that marks them as someone really rather special. Almost always they are strongly creative but with a slight lazy streak at times. It is the way they use other people in their work that brings them to the public eye. Neptune will stay in a retrograde position for over 150 days at a time usually from around March to August each year.

Pluto

Wherever this planet is found it yields an extremely deep intense and rather magnetic nature and the house or sign in which it is found will be a very strong influence. This is often someone who will not take very kindly to opposition of any kind for any reason. For as long as Pluto travels direct it gives intense power, for this means leadership – for good or ill. This planet has a slightly eccentric orbit and turns retrograde for up to 155 days at a time once a year and when stationary or travelling retrograde, Pluto inclines the subject to be more of a follower.

Finally

One final word on retrogrades with which readers may wish to experiment. Some astrologers are of the opinion that when any planet is stationary or retrograde, one should look to the house or sign opposite to the one in which it is found and read the interpretation of that house or sign as though the planet concerned were situated there. This is an interesting exercise and one that can proves to be quite revealing.

Fast or Slow

There is a rather practical and obvious (astrological) reason for people who appear to be slow in the reception and digestion of news, while others can reach the correct conclusion from the same information often before a third party has finished relating it.

All you need to do is check the speed of the Moon or on the day your subject was born. Each day the planetary movements of the heavenly bodies are listed in the Daily Motions of the Planets section of Raphael's Ephemeris but they may be just as easily worked out if you have any other kind. Write down the midday position of the Moon for the day before your time of birth and then put down that of the next noon position and subtract the lower figure from the greater.

The average daily motion of the Moon can be as slow as eleven degrees (11°) or as fast as fifteen (15°). Generally speaking, the accepted average (or mean) is 13 degrees 10 minutes (13° 10'). So, if your answer is higher than 13° 10' then the Moon is considered as fast. If your answer is less, then it is considered to be a slow Moon.

A fast-travelling Moon confers quicker perception, a more alert mind and an ability to sum up situations swiftly, although not necessarily accurately. This ability to act on such a level usually goes quite well but, just occasionally, there may be a mental block.

The Moon travelling slower than this implies an inability to assimilate new facts quickly or easily. People like this need time to absorb what is going on around them. They will then act on what they think may be the right lines and at the time although, again, not necessarily accurately.

Occasionally the speed of the inner planets, Mercury, Venus and Mars may have an effect but their influence is almost always better experienced during a transit period.

Planets "Out of Bounds"

Most "out of bounds" planets are usually found in Gemini or Cancer (northern declination) or Sagittarius and Capricorn (southern declination) but this is not set in tablets of stone. They can occur in other signs.

Any planet, more often than not the Moon, Mercury, Venus and Mars (in that order) and, occasionally, any of the outer planets that move outside of the accepted plane of the ecliptic north or south of the equator are said to be "out of bounds" (OOB).

The most usual and currently accepted limit is 23° 28" north or south of the equator. Individual planetary detail can only be verified by the ephemeris.

Planets that are out of bounds describe the ability of the subject to function "outside of the box". These positions often describe people who possess an intense need for personal freedom; lateral thinkers; original artists; people who are not bound by normal conventions and the rules of society; and sometimes those who are just plain lawless.

Perhaps one of the best examples of someone like this was Mozart who had Mars OOB at 27° N 11" at 0° Cancer. This may have described his genius, particularly as Mars was also involved in a quintile pattern (creativity).

Many modern-day astrologers have OOB planets as astrology is presently not a part of mainstream thought. This is particularly the case for astrologers who can be termed 'original thinkers' and who frequently offer new ideas or new information in astrological thinking. For the record, I have Mercury, Mars and Neptune OOB in my own birth chart. And, of course, it should go without saying that OOB planets are to be found in both natal and transit charts.

MOON OOB

Moon OOB people are likely to have very accurate intuitive moments, a deep-seated need for freedom, a strong level of self-understanding. It is easy for them to freely express their own individual feelings; they see and sense things deeply as if they had x-ray vision.

MERCURY OOB

Those with Mercury OOB just seem to never stop talking. They do have very important ideas and things to say. It can seem like a double Uranus style – with thinking and communicating out of the box.

VENUS OOB

This placement delivers a very originally creative artistic person, a genius. This aspect can also bring very strong likes and dislikes. Homosexuality can also be linked. Many people with an OOB Venus tend to become involved in or have multiple marriages. Or they may well be intentionally single. A wide age gaps between lovers/partners is often the case.

MARS OOB

This indicates deviants, criminals, outlaws, reckless, danger seekers and/or a rebel nature. OOB Mars personalities can be found as Military Generals and any role that requires total focus, dedication, and fearlessness.

Jupiter and the rest of the outer and slower planets do occasionally and quite rarely move OOB but such events are so few and far between readers need not consider them in this work. In the event of such an effect it would be mentioned within the individual forecasts.

CHAPTER SEVEN

Aries

Jupiter

Jupiter spends the first four months of 2021 in Aquarius before it moves into Pisces on 13 May 2021. So, for these first few months you must expect and will be expected to open up your social diary to the full. Other folk will show their appreciation to you and for your company. With Jupiter in this sign be ready for opportunities in both your personal life and your social commitments. With this will come a period when you will have also have the chance to influence others in ways you might not have considered before.

However, a word of warning, new romances that could come about might have a touch of the eternal triangle about them. For married people this is never a good thing while for single folk it is something you may not know about until it is too late. Nevertheless, for some singles there is a chance of marriage and, if so, you may also realise one or two of your other ambitions, should this occur. This period could also be a case of who you know rather than what you know at times.

On 13 May 2021 Jupiter enters Pisces which suggests you could further your activities as described for a short while longer. The working arena could have one or two interesting and profitable moments as well. Promotion, a transfer or a new job altogether is possible. Those people who run their own companies are likely to prosper with either new work coming in or a potential link-up with someone you know well enough to trust in such matters.

Single ladies should also find this a happier period than most.

On 28 July 2021 Jupiter slips back into Aquarius for more or less the rest of the year until 29 December 2021. This time life won't be quite as hectic and you will want a bit more time for yourself. People hitherto friendly may try to interfere with your way of life but this is something you won't tolerate from anybody. As a result, you will not only give them short shrift others will take note and stay away. Financially, you should be a tad better off. However, if you work too hard to make even more then you run the risk of damaging your health so do take care.

On 10 May 2022 Jupiter enters Aries, your own sign and will stay there until 28 October. You will feel the temptation to ride roughshod over one or two of those whom you think you can control. Equally, you may feel the urge to take chances. Think twice about this no matter how good things may look. You run the risk of heavy losses should you become too optimistic in such matters. Others will avoid you because they cannot or will not play the game your way and you could well end up on your own.

On October 29 2022 Jupiter slips back into Pisces. This will give you a breather with the chance to re-think one or two of your ideas yet again. Play it safe and think things through for what you are going to do when Jupiter moves back into Aries on 20 December 2022. This will give you five months to make your mark but with employ a much softer approach to others and to the tasks you set for yourself. Aries aren't known for their general attitude to life as a rule so this is a chance to put old errors right and make new a few new friends as you go.

On 16 May 2023 Jupiter pushes on into Taurus and stays there for a year. You will probably have to work quite a bit harder than even you might be willing to do. However, the rewards for the effort will be well worth it. This period is one where you must sustain yourself at all times. There will be opportunities to have fun here and there but the chances are that such periods are likely to coincide with the times you are needed the most. Someone has to steer the ship and, as the vessel is yours you must keep at it.

On 25 May 2024 Jupiter slips into Gemini and this should encourage your social life to increase – a sure sign of an active time for you. There might be a few ups and downs here and there on the horizon but they won't be too much trouble for you to handle if and when they do materialise. Changes, if any, will almost certainly be for the better. Many Arians are likely to become engaged while some may be actively planning their wedding. Singles could meet someone new with whom they seem to "click" straightway.

You should all enjoy the period while you can for when Jupiter moves on into Cancer on 9 June 2025 there will be a change of accent on your activities. Although Jupiter is in exaltation by sign many Aries folk may have to re-think their domestic life all round. Your job, its prospects and any potential promotion will need very careful attention at all times – perhaps more that you can or will be prepared to experience. Any changes you try to bring in might not be sufficiently good enough much later on so take care.

When Jupiter moves into Leo on 29 June 2026 it ought to presage several changes, mostly for the better. Finances should almost certainly improve sufficiently well to assist the individual to prosper whether he or she plays the stock market or just seizes opportunities as they arrive more locally. The single man or woman will also see their social and personal romantic lives open up for Jupiter in Leo almost always implies a more secure romantic life and even marriage for some.

Having enjoyed a rather helpful year or so Aries subjects will experience a few changes when Jupiter enters Virgo on 26 July 2027. This planet is a tad uncomfortable in this sign but it does help the subject to experience a few changes for the better job wise. Keep travel to a minimum and watch health and weight both of which are closely allied to the diet. If you forget this you will almost certainly have troubles in this area.

When Jupiter enters Libra just over a year later on 24 August 2028 the Aries subject will have a job keeping most things together. There will be problems in relationships, both in business and socially. Nearer to home there could be difficulties in your domestic and or conjugal issues. Thus, while there will be an opportunity for change in several areas career issues are not that good.

After 24 September 2029 Jupiter begins its journey through Scorpio which suggests money matters will improve. Cash flow problems from the previous years will ease and money from other sources, possibly abroad, will make life more bearable. Something you have started but have kept under wraps may prove to be a winner. Feelings may well run a tad deeper all year so there will be a need to become more understanding of the partner and both the older and younger members within the family circle.

Jupiter starts its passage through Sagittarius on 22 October 2030 and this will introduce all manner of improvements in the life. This is Jupiter's own sign. It will open up opportunity in career issues, the home life and travel. In some cases this might be abroad. For the singles opportunity for romance or a step up in the present relationship is likely. This will suit the older Aries people and any legal problems should be resolved in their favour.

Saturn

Saturn is in Aquarius as 2021 begins and will stay there for just over two years after which it moves into Pisces on 7 March 2023. While in Aquarius, Saturn should be fairly helpful in matters of money and, for some of those born in the early part of Aries expansion is likely. For married people it should be a relatively quiet period. Thinking and talking about or actual additions to the family are possible but one or the other partner may not be overly fond of this idea.

Saturn in Pisces implies that past events and the people concerned still worry the individual and he or she may have to take a few steps to avoid such things happening again. This does rather smack of a possible loss of opportunity. However, Saturn here often helps the individual to become more interested in the care of the less fortunate. The subject needs to become less self-involved and more positive in their overall approach to people and the world in general.

Saturn moves into Aries on 25 May 2125 and stays for around four month or so before it slides back into Pisces again on 1 September 2025. However, while the planet is in Aries people must learn to toe the line and behave accordingly. The more self-centred they become, the less they will get on with anyone – close family included. They need to develop a more positive attitude with a shade more understanding of the needs of others. Fortunately, they know how to create a much better level of self-discipline and increase the power of initiative in other folk. This should help them move forward several more steps nearer their own ambitious dreams.

On 14 February 2026 Saturn re-enters Aries. It stays there for just over two years and then moves into Taurus on 13 April 2028. Once in this sign Saturn begins to school the individual into the many ways where they can make and keep money and possessions. Those over thirty will benefit the most and many will seek promotion or a change of career where they may become even more successful. The money world will attract here: the investment field, insurance, banking and similar undertakings among them. Aries folk are natural leaders and when given their head they will become quite successful not only for themselves but also for those for whom they work as well. There is a danger of one or two folk becoming a tad miserly, so they may have to learn to be more generous in their dealings.

On 1 June 2030 Saturn enters Gemini. You should take care while travelling anywhere in any vehicle, private or otherwise, because accidents or incidents are very likely at such times. Obviously, this won't happen every time but just keep this in mind if out and about at any time. If or when writing to anyone be careful of what you write and to whom you write. Whenever you buy anything make sure you get a receipt and keep it. Generally speaking most other matters will be run-of-the-mill affairs.

Uranus

From 1 January 2021 for almost five and a half years Uranus is in Taurus and right from the start it will reveal that it and you may not fit in too well for this is the sign of its fall. Uranus likes change and will try to alter some of your ways as soon as it can. Your cooperative spirit will be taxed hard; so much so that you may have to be a tad more defensive in what you do and how you act or react at times.

You may have to develop an almost secretive way of going about some of your activities to ease any unfounded or unwanted criticism from those who ought to know better. If you get "involved" in a relationship that you should not have been allowed to start you will be found out. Uranus can be a hard task-master so remember this and you won't go far wrong.

On 7 July 2025 Uranus enters Gemini. Generally speaking most Aries subjects will have to learn through their mistakes – so often the "voice" of experience. They will have to avoid committing to a project, knowing that at the time they probably won't be able to fulfil the role they envisage. While here, Uranus helps to reshape the way Aries folk communicate and not just with people but also with the electronic or mechanical devices they have.

A few of the more open and honest types will show how practical they can be when they devise or alter the way people or systems can be organised. The older the Aries character, the more he or she will begin to change some of their ways and thinking, so that they may better fit in with everyone and everything else.

On 8 November 2025 Uranus slides back and re-enters Taurus again. It will stay there for about five months or so, then on 26 April 2026 it moves forward again into Gemini where it will stay until it enters Cancer in 2032.

Neptune

As the period begins Neptune is in Pisces and will stay there for a shade over four years when it enters Aries on 30 March 2025. While here Neptune helps to increase Aries people's appreciation of the arts. In most cases, but not always, this will be music. There will be more of an interest in the opera and or the ballet. Some plays may also. This is the natural 12th house for Aries folk and, as a rule, these subjects may begin to take more of an interest in the super-natural. For some, this could lead to Free-Masonry while for others it might mean delving a little more into the so-called hidden side of life.

There may well be a desire for more seclusion from the usual daily grind which, in turn, might incline the individual to become a difficult person to get to know, live or work with at times. At the very least, he or she will seek a more peaceful existence and not socialise too much especially where it is noisy.

On 30 March 2025 Neptune enters your own sign of Aries. This will mark an increase in the understanding of many things but in the more mundane world he or she will become quite active in pioneering new or different ways of getting things done both at work or in the home. Intuition is likely to become stronger and there will be a clearly defined and obvious impressionism in life generally.

New friends will be made and gradually there may be a change in the way in which you socialise. There is a danger of drinking and or just playing with drugs at times. Some turn to a form of what most people would call "loose-living", although this is not really in the Aries nature, as a rule. A touch of selfishness may also develop.

About six month later on 22 October 2025 Neptune re-enters Pisces for about three months. While in retrograde motion here the planet is influential in the way the subject develops his or her growing interest with past events and or people from their past. There may also be an inclination to become emotionally "involved" with another partner or start a secret liaison that might be frowned upon or that could be interpreted as an "eternal triangle" association.

On 26 January 2026 Neptune moves back into Aries again and will stay there until 2038. This will help the subject develop his or her initiative in many ways. However, they must also learn that their ideas are not necessarily shared by other folk and any attempt to become too dogmatic will hold them back at work and socially.

Pluto

As 2021 opens Pluto is in Capricorn. This is a rather useful placing for it helps to endow Aries people with more ambition for a higher position within the company that they are employed. However, in this they must be careful not to become overly ambitious or status conscious. Further, they must also remember how to speak to other employees or more senior staff properly. Big business, the financial fields and politics in all its aspects will probably attract. Once again, for as long as the Aries person approaches people in the proper manner he or she will succeed.

Aries people who have Pluto in this, their natural tenth house, will see their ambitions, hopes and ideals vastly strengthened. It might well be someone from this sign who could (would) be able to start a new political party. It is a racing certainty that they would also insist on for a freedom from the old ways of doing things as a matter of high priority. Pluto here helps to re-shape the individuals' overall approach of doing things. Somehow or another they are likely to develop a much better organised way of life. However, a word of warning is due here because if they do get caught out doing anything wrong their fall from grace will not go unnoticed. They almost certainly won't be able to regain the top ground again.

On March 23 2023 Pluto edges into Aquarius to stay there for about six or seven weeks. This "taster" of a visit to this sign and house placement prior to a much longer stay later in the period under review will herald the start of the making of a quite different type of person. The accent here is on personal freedom first and foremost and also freedom from any restrictive practices brought about by politics or government's pressure that that may be exerted on the people.

There are those who would try to impose their will in other areas away from government, political or business affairs. Should this occur, those who seek such power will fail and their standing in whatever community they may dwell. When this sort of ability is channelled into the more practical concerns of life – business, science, technology and so on, there can be little to prevent success. But, it does take a lot of hard work.

On June 11 2023 Pluto re-enters Capricorn again to remain there for about six months or so. Pluto then changes signs again on 11 Jan 2024 and ventures back into Capricorn for around a seven to an eight month stay. This will be a flying visit as such for a few weeks later on 19 November 2024 Pluto edges forward to re-enter Aquarius again but this time for quite a long stay – until 9 March 2043.

During this long period all manner of challenges will be met – especially by Aries folk for this planet will now be a long-term fixture in their 11th house. There will be much original thinking and strong relationships created and built up in all areas of life.

CHAPTER EIGHT

Taurus

Jupiter

As the year 2021 opens, Jupiter is in Aquarius but only for about five months. While the planet is here it helps people realise that too much self-will and, on occasions, intolerance is not the right way to get things done either in the home, socially or in the business sector. Most set-backs, therefore, will be of the Taurus person's own fault. Some family issues will need careful handling, perhaps with the wisdom of Job at times. It is largely a favourable period when sudden changes in the career or business life could come about; setbacks from which it might take a long time to recover.

On the other hand, some of the changes may be quite electric and catapult you into areas you have hitherto only dreamed about. Married Taurus folk might not get the support from their respective spouses that they think they are due.

On May 13 2021 Jupiter enters Pisces for a very short stay. Jupiter in the eleventh house can be quite a profitable area for most Taurus born folk. Unfortunately, there is a possibility of some underhand dealings in which the subject will use other folk for his or her personal advancement. Whatever their personal feelings might seem to be the Taurean is likely to become a tad too extravagant and more than a shade unreliable.

On July 28 2021 Jupiter slides back into Aquarius for more or less the rest of the year. During these five months a noticeable change will show as he or she becomes more open and honest in the way they get along with other folk whatever their position or persuasion. Also, as time moves on, they should become more open and less insistent on status.

On 29 December 2021 Jupiter re-enters Pisces again. Lessons will have been learned and now Taurus folk should be able to enjoy a more enlightened five months or so. By now they will or should have seen that a more tolerant approach to all and sundry are more or less essential in private, social and business life.

On 10 May 2022 Jupiter enters Aries, your 12th house, and will stay there for around six months or so.

Quite a few Taurus folk will be inclined to show a more friendly face to those with whom they have been having troubles. Friendships could come about with such people as they both enter a new understanding of each other and their wants and needs. For a few there may well be a new attitude grow toward the less fortunate in this world.

One or two of the younger Taurus people may try to hold down two jobs at once and, if this should occur any mistakes made could cost them dearly – and not just in monetary terms.

On 28 October 2022 Jupiter slips back into Pisces for about six weeks. This temporary 11th house placement implies a new interest in technical matters but, by the time Taurus folk take for this to sink in Jupiter again moves forward into Aries on 20 December 2022. If nothing else, they ought to develop a shade more tolerance and broadmindedness.

Some five months later Jupiter moves into your own sign and first house on 16 May 2023. While here in Taurus the planet influences the subject to be a tad more self-indulgent and will probably help to increase personal assets with some better-class purchases sought mostly for the home. These people will also lean toward a better social life while at the same time they will try to improve their status within the community.

A year later on 25 May 2024 Jupiter will move into Gemini for about a year's stay. Once the greater benefic is in your second house life will improve. Your business abilities will become more astute, connections will be made with those who will not only help but also share in your good fortune. The thing to watch out for here is that you do not take too much for granted. The watchword here is for you to pay attention to detail.

Taurus folk are likely to become a tad restless and will turn to all manner of things they haven't yet dabbled in to see if they can make use of whatever catches their eye. Communication of all kinds will almost certainly reach the top of this list. There could be a half interest (or possibly a shade more) with respect to redecorating, moving home or buying another house.

On 9 June 2025 Jupiter enters Cancer. This planet is exalted in the 3rd house of Taurus which means it is comfortable and performs quite well. So, for the next year a lot of good can come of this. Local social activities together with the associated life style will increase. More travel is indicated, more than likely to do with work but nothing too extreme. The offspring of married couples will look for advice and guidance. This will bring home to those whose children have not yet left home that the time may not be that far off for when they do.

Jupiter begins to transit Leo on 30 June 2026. In this Taurus 3rd house the planet will start to influence a more expansive look at life. Family relationships will strengthen where they might have been a little on the weak side before. There may even be a little more travel than the previous year which might involve promotion or a change of position. Taurus folk should expect their lives to involve meeting and making new friends, activities and interests otherwise a streak of boredom is liable to set in. You might take up an interest you have always had in a possible alternative hobby.

Jupiter enters Virgo on 26 July 2027. Taurus folk will have a good, reasonably thirteen months or so and may even throw their home open for people to come and meet together in a mutual interest. For some, matters of health, diet and general well-being will need attention. Almost everything that does take place in any area of life will be subjected to far more attention to detail – in extreme cases this might even become a tad over the top and invite criticism from those close to them.

Jupiter in Virgo is not always an entirely comfortable position for Taurus folk. Any inclination to try to branch out to work on your own should be seriously thought about because, quite honestly and at the present time, you will do far better as part of a team no matter how big it may be or become.

On 24 August 2028 Jupiter moves on and edges into Libra where it will stay for thirteen months. There will always be the temptation to pass odd jobs and work on to other people but there will be times when you would much rather play your cards close to your chest. Either way, try not to fall foul of becoming indulgent. You will start to be scrupulously fair in your dealings with other people and there will be an ever increasing dislike of injustice. The younger folk looking or wanting a suitable career might enrol in one of the caring professions such as medicine. The older Taurus people are likely to develop more responsibility within their working arena.

Jupiter enters Scorpio on 24 September 2029. When here the planet inclines Taurus folk to think seriously about their role in life and how they may be viewed by to others. They start to be more open, friendly and much more accessible than in recent times. He or she is likely to flourish in business matters and some could even start their own. Marriage, if any, could take place with someone who is of a better standing socially or financially.

You might also become a tad too trusting so be careful because you could so easily be caught up in scams which could be quite costly. Unless specifically trained otherwise, don't pursue the hidden world of the unknown because you might easily become rather susceptible in this area. Jupiter in Scorpio inclines the individual to be sympathetic in this respect. Try to remember that there are rather more charlatans in this area than you might expect.

Jupiter moves into Sagittarius on 22 October 2030. In the few weeks to the end of the year, it will not have had a chance to influence anything. In the coming months, however, there will be an increased interest in foreign affairs. Your overall attitude to all forms of money matters will gradually begin to change and this will go on until Jupiter enters the next sign in November 2031.

Saturn

As the period under review opens Saturn is in Aquarius, your tenth house, until early March 2023. The overall inclination will be to look at things in a far more practical manner than before. A love of justice and fair-mindedness will increase. Your social life should open up; perhaps allied to business and work issues and your ambitions will grow. As this all happens you may also grow a tad more emotional with an air of selfishness possibly creeping in. There is likely to be a couple of occasions when you may totally "blank" one or two of your friends or associates because of how you view what they seem to have become involved in. It might not be what they have actually done but how you see the matter from your point of view.

It is worth noted here that Saturn is exalted in this house and especially so this time because Aquarius rules your tenth house of ambition, work and standing in the community. There will be an ever-growing desire to better your status but if you do anything wrong or underhand to achieve this end you will have a fall from grace from which you might never recover. This will become more so if you should dabble in politics.

On 7 March 2023 Saturn moves on into Pisces, your eleventh house, for a shade more than two years. It is important that you realise Saturn constricts, plays down and wants the most sensible, practical and responsible attitude to all that you want to do. So, you will lean more and more to the "right" way of applying your abilities but you won't become involved in anything underhand. You might even become a tad introspective at times – holding back until you have made up your mind what you are going or ought to do for the best. You will gravitate toward older and influential types who will show you the right and proper way to act and react.

On 25 May 2025 Saturn enters Aries, your twelfth house for about three months or so. You will begin to learn to look after yourself even more and will become quite resourceful. There may be just enough time to get used to some of the effect of Saturn here because on 1 September 2025 the planet regresses back into Pisces for about five 5 months.

On February 14 2026 Saturn re-enters Aries again to stay for just over two years. Just remember that to really succeed you must be aware of what those with whom you work and play want from life. Their needs and ideas on life may not be the same as yours so try not to be too controlling and let them do whatever they when they want. It won't be easy but you will feel the benefits if you behave yourself in this area.

On 1 June 2028 Saturn enters Taurus to stay for just over two years. Saturn is in its fall here, that is, not quite as strong an influence as it might be elsewhere. Irrespective of this, you will be inclined to be rather responsible and even a shade too austere in some of the things you become involved in. The older Taurus man or woman will seek out more ambitious positions or status because they "know" they can vindicate themselves given the opportunity. At the same time, these people will become more independent which in itself is not a problem but being uncooperative is. This is one danger that you must avoid at all costs or your personal popularity will suffer.

On 1 June 2030 Saturn enters Gemini where it will stay for much longer than this period under review. Once here, however, your financial arrangements should start to help you to accrue the better things of life that you feel should be yours by right which, in your case, would be by your achievements. At about this time many Taurus folk often consider teaching or instructional work of some kind.

Uranus

As 2021 opens Uranus is in Taurus in its fall, your first house, and where it will stay until the middle of 2025. This planet influences change which is likely to happen quite suddenly. While in Taurus it will instil more liking for musical appreciation and artistic ability. Taurus people will seek and probably achieve a lot more freedom in or with whatever they may become involved. While reasonably comfortable financially and in other material ways a few Taureans are likely to become interested in gambling. This may be for just a few pounds here and there in most cases but with some it might become a far more serious affair.

Behaviour patterns may lean toward rather erratic moments, often quite unpredictably so. Friends, associates and business colleagues could be taken quite aback at times – so, take care. Feelings of restlessness will develop especially when you get so easily bored. You may well branch out into things you nothing about but might have always wanted to try. You will also develop a level of flexibility in some ways while in others you are likely to become a tad too stubborn especially for those close to you.

On 7 July 2025 Saturn moves on into Gemini for about three months. A sense of mistrust may develop but this will be easily offset by a kind of new-found business acumen along with an ability to make money. If you were restless before, you are liable to become even more so at this time but this may not gather any real momentum because on 8 Nov 2025 Saturn will re-enter Taurus for about three months or so.

There should not be great deal of change at this time because only a short while later on 26 April 2026 Saturn moves once more into Gemini where it will stay until far beyond 2030. This position in Gemini will cause you to try to travel a little more than usual. It matters little whether this will comprise short journeys or long-distance affairs. As long as you can get away from familiar surroundings occasionally, you will feel a lot better in yourself.

Neptune

As 2021 starts the great planet Neptune is in Pisces, your eleventh house where it will stay until 30 March 2025. This rather slow moving outer planet feels at home here and will create an even greater interest and liking for the arts in general. It will help you make new friends several of whom are a part and parcel of these activities. You will become more relaxed in your ways generally especially with how you get along with other folk. Any humanitarian tendencies will become greatly strengthened.

Single Taurus people will tend to be very selective, choosy almost, in their choice of partner. They do so dislike having to change in this area. On the other hand, would-be partners often think twice before they let themselves get involved with people while Neptune is in Pisces. On the other hand they are also aware of how steady Taurus folk can be. This could be a "sticky" business for those who find themselves so attracted.

On 30 March 2025 Neptune makes an initial foray into Aries for about six months. This will create a rather sensitive soul altogether. He or she may start to feel many of the old ways of achieving things are the best and a sense of traditionalism may set in a few folk. Often, the best place for such people is to work either alone or in the background where they can get along with whatever they want to do at their own pace and ability.

However, much before anything really concrete gets under way Neptune reverses its role and re-enters Pisces on 22 October 2025 for about three months. As there are no serious aspects to worry about here, very little will influence Taurus people until Neptune changes direction once more and re-enters Aries on 26 January 2026 where it will stay until 2038.

Pluto

From 1 January 2021 Pluto will be in and out of just two signs and houses throughout the ten years. It opens the decade in Capricorn to stay for over two years. While it is in the ninth house for Taurus the planet will start to influence the way you think and talk about your opinions and beliefs. This could bring about some tough talking at times and is bound to lead to arguments. Anything new or (possibly) untried you will view with some doubts from time to time.

You are likely to develop a sense adventure in some areas and, as a result, you may meet with quite a few new people and experiences. This could lead into some kind of instructional or teaching work. Another benefit from this (depending on your viewpoint) is that you are more likely to become involved in a lot more travel than usual. This will either lead you into new things altogether or extend your present understanding of what you have come to know so far.

On 23 March 2023 Pluto moves into Aquarius, the tenth house in your chart. It will stay here for less than three months and then edge back into Capricorn again on 11 June 2023 this time to stay for just on six months. On 21 January 2024 it again moves into Aquarius for an eight month stay. After this apparent "breather" Pluto moves once again into Capricorn on 1 September 2024. It then re-enters Aquarius on 19 November 2024 and remains there until 2043.

While in this sign and house Pluto will exert its influence in several areas of your life. You will begin to stand out more as you push hard to achieve your ambitions or pursue your aims with more determination. Research work might attract perhaps to improve the way some things are carried out in the work arena.

A particularly strong sense of responsibility will begin to show but if you are up against tradition you should at least tread with some care even if you think such things are out of date. A few Taurus folk will become extremely detail orientated and will prefer to be a leader rather than a follower.

CHAPTER NINE

Gemini

Jupiter

Jupiter is in Aquarius for the first four months or so of 2021. Travel, communication perhaps linked in with business requirements should feature strongly. Some Gemini folk will actually go abroad for the first time later this year. Money matter matters and the Geminian should find him or herself in a much better all-round situation than before.

Jupiter enters Pisces on 13 May 2021. Overall, the career and the working arena generally should be looking quite rosy for this planet is now in Gemini's tenth house although this will only be for a few weeks because on 28 July 2021 Jupiter moves back into Aquarius for just on five months. Gemini folk may develop what appears to be a rather brusque nature but this should ease up for the rest of the year.

On 29 December 2021 Jupiter moves once more into Pisces. This will increase the confidence of others who have to deal with Gemini people at whatever level they may be in. Family life may become a tad fraught with a problem that ought not to arise perhaps to deal more with relatives than anything deeply personal. Domestic relationships will need delicate handling; married couples could have their work cut out trying to overcome these issues.

Jupiter moves into Aries on May 10 2022 for just over four months. The greatest temptation here is that some Gemini folk will try too hard and probably take on far more than they can handle. When they over-reach themselves like this instead of easing back and asking for help they are likely to become a tad rash and an even impulsive as they try to put things right.

On 28 October 2022 Jupiter retrogrades back into Pisces for a few weeks and re-enters Aries on 20 December 2022 where it will be for six months. While in this eleventh house of Gemini Jupiter will try to influence these people into a better spirit of cooperation and social life in general. What Gemini must not do is not to take anyone or anything for granted.

On 16 May 2023 Jupiter enters Taurus and will be here for a year. Gemini is naturally curious about anything they don't quite understand. The coming twelve months or so will be almost a seventh heaven for them as or if they probe here and there into all sorts of things. Also, many Gemini subjects are likely to make and break quite a few friendships as they get involved. A spirit of leadership and control (which they love) will start to develop as they begin to emerge as good candidates for promotion or special jobs that they should be able to handle with one hand tied behind their back.

On 25 May 2024 Jupiter edges into Gemini to stay for a year. This ought to favour just about all Gemini men and women everywhere. This will be a time of growth and a time of making many new friends and associates socially and in business. Their standing will be quite high for this is a time of hard work with all the accompanying rewards. Those about to choose a career (the younger element mostly) which demands a period of study first are likely to opt for teaching, the law and medicine. In a few cases the church may be preferred.

Jupiter begins a transit of Cancer on 9 June 2025. Gemini folk will have need of or will perhaps take up a position in real estate, the food industry, domestic products or publishing. In the last mentioned world many Gemini people do quite well when they really apply themselves. In this, the second house of Gemini, possessions and earnings will become quite important. It won't be so much as how much they have but in what they do with it. A gambling streak may develop and should be resisted at all times for they are liable to well over-step the mark.

The great planet begins its journey through Leo on 30 June 2026. Gemini people will begin to flourish well at all kinds of social arrangements but should learn to avoid the really lavish affairs because their pockets are only so deep. Some will begin or turn to business matters to do with entertainment, sport or any of the background industries associated with such things. More travel is possible and relationships with siblings and or local people should grow much stronger.

On 26 July 2027 Jupiter enters Virgo. While Jupiter isn't exactly confortable in the sign it is virtually at home here because it is accidentally exalted in the fourth house. This is almost certainly going to produce one or two "push-me / pull-you" moments for many Gemini folk. Such situations must be dealt with as they arrive because the longer they are left the worse they will become. Think twice about opening the home to others for meetings of any sort. Concern with too much detail and not enough common sense could bring a few problems.

On 24 August 2028 Jupiter moves into Libra. People in sales forces will really become quite a force to deal with; they could sell snow to Eskimos for this is going to be their year always provided they apply themselves to the task(s) at hand. Some will become a tad too reliant on those around them while others could go to the other extreme and adopt a totally independent way of life altogether. Single folk may find this a good year for a new partner while married couples should grow closer to one another. Children and their needs may become expensive at times. Try not to extend yourself too much or you could incur considerable losses, and if in business there is a danger of bankruptcy.

Jupiter enters Scorpio on 24 September 2029. This period will create emotional intensity but in such a way as to cause others to view them in a totally different light. If Gemini people behave themselves and make the effort, this could be a great year in their working arena. Popularity would go with this quite easily. A few could end up mediating between warring workers because both sides in such matters trust their judgement and abilities in this area.

Jupiter moves on into Sagittarius on 22 October 2030. The social life will start to grow possibly with a sporting flavour to it. Outdoor activities will attract where in all likelihood animals are involved. But this is a very short time to the end of the period under review and what has been suggested here will take a little longer than what is left of 2030.

Saturn

Saturn is in Aquarius as 2021 opens and will be there for a shade over two years. Saturn in the 9th house of Gemini implies a rather fastidious sort of person who knows how to handle money; their own and that of others. This placing will also influence a more practical outlook and way of life. However, these people may become hard to get to know. Unless you have good reason not to, you should appeal to them with facts and not emotion. Any business or professional activities should tend to incline them toward the legal world and publishing. Such work may also mean more travel than usual.

Saturn enters Pisces on 7 March 2023 to stay for just over two years and is accidentally exalted because the tenth house corresponds with Capricorn and is the ruling planet of that sign. So, in such a powerful position this will lead to an inclination to achieve or to want to better oneself. Geminians over 30 are likely to succeed, while the younger element here will try to ensure they work hard to attain their aims. It won't be all work and no play for when these people do relax they make sure they enjoy themselves. They make good friends and, for as long as you are loyal to them they will be equally so to you. They may well become more socially orientated but it will be with people who matter and who can do things for them.

Saturn moves into Aries on 25 May 2025 and while in this eleventh house of Gemini Saturn tries to create more social life out of the individual. This will suit Gemini because he or she will be attracted to someone a tad older with a little more experience of life; someone who is settled. Gemini people will exhibit a lot more independence than usual. However, at the same time they probably won't show a great deal of consideration for those around them, especially at work. Saturn is in its fall in this sign so Gemini people of both sexes and all ages will have to work hard just to maintain their status quo to which they have become quite used.

On 1 September 2025 Saturn retrogrades back into Pisces to stay for about five months or so. Gemini men and women will once again see chances to be able to chase up their aims in business affairs but this won't last too long for Saturn will move back into Aries on 14 February 2026 which is likely to lead them to be a shade less comfortable but still able to pursue their dreams.

On 13 April 2028 Saturn enters Taurus. Once in this twelfth house of Gemini the subjects will start to be influenced to become more reliable. They will become more detail conscious and rather well controlled and controlling for those about them in the working arena. One or two may have health problems where weight and diet are concerned. Generally speaking, Geminians are normally a shade more frugal when Saturn is placed here. Possessions will become important and when out purchasing anything only the best is likely to satisfy them. It would be helpful if they could develop an outdoor hobby or pursuit of some kind to offset some of this more serious approach to life.

On 1 June 2030 Saturn edges into Gemini and stays there until July 2032. Once in their own sign this planet does tend to make the subject even more serious minded and practical beyond reasonable expectations. They could lose some friends because of this. There could be other losses on some occasions through this period. There may well be money matters of some kind that will need careful consideration. This could be their own money or that which others may have entrusted to them. Heavier bills than usual are likely to come through the post. In this period the Gemini individual tend to shine in engineering, mechanical or allied business areas. However, whatever work they do or become involved with, they must be very careful when creating contracts or writing other paperwork. They are liable to errors which could cost them quite dearly later.

Uranus

As the period under review opens Uranus is in Taurus for their next five years. There will be an underlying period of wondering what might happen next long before it does if, indeed, it ever anything does come about. One could describe this as someone trying to cross his or her bridges long before there would be any need to do so. Uranus here implies the subject is likely to feel or become increasingly lonely or unable to talk or mix properly with other people. Taurus is a fixed sign which might make Gemini subjects seem to be a tad more decisive than usual. However, this may not be so for Gemini people are so easy going as a rule. On another tack altogether, Uranus here will help Gemini folk come up with a lot more new and, possibly, highly original ideas in monetary matters. This could involve the use of computers which for these people ought to be almost a second nature for them.

On 7 July 2025 Uranus moves into Gemini and the first house. After some five years of having to hold back, or be unable to express their ideas easily Uranus here will enhance their role in their social life and business matters. There will be a danger of over-doing things occasionally and this will lead to some restlessness and a potentially weakened health state. Gemini positively hates indecision – their own or that of anyone else. Routine is another sore point with these people. They often seem ready for what might happen rather than what does actually occur. With all this in mind, be prepared for any Geminian friend to become a tad unpredictable at times. Watch them start to play hardball as they struggle to achieve more influence in any group or business circle within which they move. Uranus here implies Gemini on fire trying to get somewhere rather than stand still where they have always been.

Uranus retreats back into Taurus on 8 November 2025. This will be a short stay of some six months or so and the planet will be retrograde most of the time until it turns direct again on 3

Feb 2026. When retrograde, Uranus in the twelfth house inclines people to be tempted to take chances to attain his or her aim. If their career takes them behind the scenes in their work they will have to learn to control their temper because it will seem get more and more on a short leash. While this period may not last long enough for anything serious to occur they must be careful of any possible damage they might do within their social and or business relationships.

On 26 April 2026 Uranus moves on again into Gemini. Beware potential rather than actual marital disagreements that could lead initially to separation. If this is not for just a short while then divorce might be looming on the horizon. However, that is the worst that can happen. The alternative will be a number of short "spats" which will be resolved one way or another. Travel may well be higher than usual on the Gemini agenda. Such travel may be for short or long journeys for either pleasure of business purposes.

Neptune

As the period under review opens up Neptune will be in Pisces.

For the next ten years Neptune will be in Pisces, the natural 10th house for Gemini folk and, while in Aries it will occupy the Geminian 11th house. When Neptune transits the natural tenth house of Gemini it often points to an unusual career and even more so if this career should change during this period. Neptune makes us think of ourselves and the greater perspective, the spiritual and the mystical side of life. Some will gravitate toward the film and or entertainment world where they would do well in promotional and publicity work. For some Gemini people the more mundane aspects of life do sometimes attract. They may exhibit a few strange ideas and practices when they do but, by and large and unless you (verbally) attack these beliefs you should mutually enjoy a great relationship.

On 30 March 2025 Neptune enters Aries, the eleventh house for Gemini. Once the planet has had a chance to settle in you will become all fired up with all sorts of new ideas and schemes mostly to do with either the main career or with whatever else occupies your mind when not working. Any new friends made during this period need to be carefully selected. Make sure they are not around to use you, your talents or contacts. Curiously, you may also do something along these lines yourself only you will look for those who are older than you, and therefore more experienced in what you may be seeking. Your sense of humour will become quite keen but could be a tad cutting on occasions. A word of warning: no matter what you may be interested in at the time never, ever jump in with both feet especially if you have only recently met your (or any) advisor. Always wait for a little while you check things out for yourself. There are a lot of "scam" artists about these days.

Neptune turns retrograde on 4 July 2025 and re-enters Pisces on 22 October 2025. Neptune won't be here that long to create any serious problems but any contacts with your partner's family members could become hard to handle; it would be best to keep a low profile in this area. Further, should there be anything new in your family life, social obligations or work that demands close attention must be taken care of so read the details or rules carefully.

Neptune re-enters Aries once more on 26 January 2026 to stay there until 2038. These large and slow moving planets have more of a generational influence as against anything else when in transit. But, having made the point, Neptune in Aries will have some effect. There is a danger of becoming a shade too confident in your own abilities. Try to be as open as you can at all times because you are also likely to become more sensitive than usual. People in the entertainment field should see their career prospects improve. Background workers could be in line for a transfer, promotion or a different job altogether.

Pluto

As the period under review opens Pluto is in Capricorn. Between now and the end of 2030 this planet will be in either Capricorn, the Gemini eighth house or Aquarius, the ninth house. It moves several times and we will deal with them in turn.

While in transit in Capricorn this rather slow moving outer planet only registers a slight overall effect. Gemini people are likely to become more heavily involved in money matters, their own and or that of others. There is a risk of failing to meet certain demands by "manipulating" what assets you do have. For single people of either sex co-habitation or even marriage is possible. The career arena also looks quite promising.

On 23 March 2023 Pluto enters Aquarius. While here Pluto will engage you in re-shaping some of your overall character outlook the outcome of which will help create a more approachable nature. On the downside, you may "bend" a few rules to get your own way.

Pluto will hardly be here for anything solid or definite to take place because the plant retrogrades back into Capricorn on 11 June 2023. Some six month later on 21 January 2024 Pluto edges back into Aquarius again. Barely eight months later, Pluto returns into Capricorn on 1 September 2024 where it will be for just a few weeks, for it then advances back into Aquarius again on 19 November 2024 to stay until 2043.

CHAPTER TEN

Cancer

Jupiter

Jupiter is in Aquarius for the first four months or so of 2021 and it looks quite good for the most part. When you come to deal with other people treat them as equals because while it will make them feel better they will also tend to work well. However, any interplay between managers and employees is not always easy or that straightforward. Do be careful if or when entering into any large contracts where money is concerned then there should be few if any problems in this area. Legal issues of all kinds should be dealt with by the right people; don't let things like this go by the board without proper control.

Jupiter enters Pisces on 18 May 2021. This suggests money matters will flourish and more travel is a possibility. This could be linked in with your working arena. You may be asked to set up a department for instructional purposes or start some extra curricula re self-education. Emotional matters go well, and younger folk may begin a courtship leading to a long-term relationship.

On 28 July Jupiter retrogrades back into Aquarius for a few months. It will depend on any aspects to the contrary but you may have to put one or two of your working plans on hold; however, this should not be too much of a problem.

Jupiter re-enters Pisces again on 29 December 2021. This should give you an opportunity to start a few of your favourite ideas back on the move again. For some, a stronger interest in religious or affiliated interests may start up. Some charity-based work perhaps.

Jupiter moves into Aries on 22 May 2022 for a short while. On 28 October 2022 the planet reverts back into Pisces again for just a few weeks. In these two short periods Cancerians of both sexes will have the chance to take on a spare time occupation. It may be something where other folk might need their services. It might not last long but it might throw up a few ideas for something elsewhere.

Jupiter re-enters Aries on 20 December 2022. A few Cancerians born in the first ten degrees or so of the sign will see improvements in the way they work. This may be a promotion, a transfer or something completely new. Tread a tad carefully for a little while for it may not all be as it seems at first. The chance of a loss of some kind is indicated.

On 16 May 2023 Jupiter enters Taurus. Here in the eleventh house of Cancer there is a suggestion of being able to accrue and enjoy new acquisitions. There will be a need to monitor diet and health because most Cancerians are liable to overdo such things, once they get the bit under their teeth.

On 25 May 2024 Jupiter edges into Gemini to stay for a year. This will help to increase their level of versatility and the opportunity for them to dabble in whatever takes their fancy – the mark of a true Cancerian. Some will opt for working or even being on their own more. The younger element could decide to enter into a writing career of some kind such as journalism perhaps.

Jupiter begins a transit of Cancer on 9 June 2025 which is good for it is in exaltation here. Most Cancerians will flourish in just about everything they attempt. Many will become more socially minded and the older the subject the more this may be so. Young Cancerians can look forward to quite a bit of help from their parents, always assuming the older folk approve of what is on their mind. Bad aspects by transit could incline the subject to promise more than they can deliver.

The great planet begins its journey through Leo on 30 June 2026. And once in the second house more business acumen is likely. The major fault is that the subject can get carried away with any success. A love of all the good things in life will increase even more so, once again, diet and health must be carefully monitored. Vanity is also a possible enemy to have to fight.

On 26 July 2027 Jupiter enters Virgo. Marriage prospects for the single people of either sex look quite promising. During this transit Many Cancerians are likely to become more detail minded in just about all they do. Generally speaking this ought to be quite a busy period for local activities. An interest in politics could develop. The personal appearance may undergo a change. At work, these people must learn how to delegate more efficiently. Don't put off anything today to be done tomorrow.

On 24 August 2028 Jupiter moves into Libra. A hint of a lazy streak is liable to set in and you may tend to sit back and hope that one or two adverse moments might just go away but this won't happen. Justice and fair play will play its part this year. The more reliant you try be with others, the more trouble you are likely to bring on yourself. Curb the lazy streak before it gets too tight a hold. The home and family life will play a strong role around this period.

Jupiter enters Scorpio on 24 September 2029. A rather material outlook will develop along with a shrewd business flair as well. Do have people help out if or when it becomes necessary because you might be surprised at just how useful they could be in other matters with which you are involved. You will become more sensitive and if you have children a tad over-protective in some of their plans and ambitions. Young Cancerians will develop romantic interests.

Jupiter moves on into Sagittarius on 22 October 2030. In this short period outdoor life and interests are likely to develop along with a more matter-of-fact and practical outlook.

Saturn

Saturn is in Aquarius as 2021 opens. Money matters could prove to be a tad difficult at times with delays, losses and un-kept promises especially from those who owe money might also feature. None of this is going to help your overall outlook and there is a chance of becoming selfish and more sensitive emotionally. Ambitions will grow and intensify, if and or when the opportunity for moving comes your way. Justice and fair play will become important and, should you go to court for any reason you should seek professional help rather than try to do it yourself.

Saturn enters Pisces on 7 March 2023. Business when travel might become important and changes will also feature during this period. Don't take chances because accidents could occur when you least expect them and almost always at the wrong time. In other matters long term agreements of some kind could come to fruition. Try not to re-live past glories or other events from the past. Instead, try to develop a more positive attitude in the present. The overall personality is likely to become more tolerant in some issues but in others you will prove to a rather formidable foe if challenged.

Saturn moves into Aries on 25 May 2025 which is not a good place for the planet is in its fall in this sign. However, it might also be the most elevated planet in the chart at times, so a lot of good can come of this. Remember timing will be of an essence in many Cancerian activities. Saturn here also favours decisiveness in business and political issues. It also suggests resourcefulness will be rewarded along with ambition. For some, there is a possible fall from grace but that will depend if or when your attitude and ability is called into question and you have been found wanting.

On 1 September 2025 Saturn retrogrades back into Pisces and, for this short period, any positional advance offered should be rejected because you probably won't be up to it.

Saturn moves into Aries again on 14 February 2026 for a few short weeks but there is hardly any time for any effects to take place. However, if promotion or a transfer is offered you should accept it because you will make a success of it. This will not be immediately but in the long run.

On 13 April 2028 Saturn enters Taurus. Young people will have to learn the hard way for as they grow up they must also become more responsible and Saturn here is the right planet to ensure this. Discipline and hard work will also be needed for all Cancerians irrespective of their age. One or two friends may disappoint even though they may be working for Cancer people's benefit at the time. Money matters matter but not during this period, for losses may ensue. Best not to start anything new and that goes for romance too. It might be better to accept what you have now and wait for more rewarding times later.

On 1 June 2030 Saturn edges into Gemini. Saturn here implies problems from sources that won't be immediately obvious at the time. However, once you do find out who is causing you trouble you will certainly know precisely how to deal with them. The teaching profession may attract the younger Cancerian looking for a possible career for him or her to pursue. The older people may feel a tad too settled and might want to try to do things they either used to do or always wanted to do. For some, this will be a mistake, for a few it will totally be wrong. A handful may have a modicum of success as long as they approach whatever it is with plenty of common sense.

Uranus

As the period under review opens Uranus will be in Taurus and will remain there for the next five years. It is accidentally dignified here in Cancer's eleventh house but traditional thinkers won't be all that keen. Uranus here calls for a matter-of-fact modern approach to all that is wanted. Good Cancerians are noted for their fairness as a rule but many seem to have a more impersonal approach to people and tasks in general. Younger folk who have or who adopt a similar approach will not have much luck in romantic entanglements. At work (or at play for some) computers and similar gadgets are likely to play a bigger role than usual. It would be rather helpful if these people appreciate that planning and practicality should go hand in hand.

On 7 July 2025 Uranus moves into Gemini. Cancerians are going to feel rather restless as they try to settle down with what they have or with the plans they may be hatching for their future. The only problem now is that they must try to develop sensible ideas to work with but they will tend to get a shade impractical because they don't (can't or won't) take the time to think things through properly. It would be a good idea to be ready to counter those ready to criticise their actions. A flair for the way they communicate with others will start to grow. Those involved in teaching or instructing others must learn to relax more. They should not expect too much from those who have had to learn at least some of what they have been able to do for so long. This may create a few difficult moments so do try to be reasonable if or when this might happen.

Uranus retreats back into Taurus on 8 November 2025. During this period and because Uranus is a very slow moving influence in the heavens, Cancerians should not become too aggrieved if anything should go wrong at times. A retrograde Uranus often runs away with things and creates all manner of sudden changes that the average individual just wasn't expecting – but then that is how Uranus acts quite a lot of the time. The planet will turn direct again on 3 Feb 2026. In this short period of time the planet will have had very little, if any influence on anything.

Once back in Gemini on 28 April 2028 any of the old negative issues will be dealt with quite deftly. Cancerians will have had to have learned a few Gemini tricks such as being sufficiently inventive and original to thwart those who would oppose them. Despite the obvious difference between the Gemini subjects and the Cancerian people our subject in this time spell won't have a lot to worry about. Most will probably be ready for whatever Lady Luck might want to throw at them.

However, a word of warning will be helpful here. Travel will attract quite a lot now and there will be times when just to relieve their love of making long or short journeys a few Cancerians are likely to let their restlessness get the better of them and take themselves off to here, there or anywhere just to alleviate the problem. This will be a time when those who would oppose could strike. Do make sure all is secure if you should be away at any time.

Neptune

As the period under review opens up Neptune will be in Pisces and for the next ten years Neptune will be in Pisces and or Aries one way or another. So, when in Pisces, which is the Cancer subject's ninth house many will find their most personal attitudes, desires, needs and wants are liable to undergo a few changes. Some will be good while others certainly won't be and people especially close to them might have trouble getting along with them.

Neptune is more of a generation planet than anything else but on occasions it does affect the subjects often quite severely. During this period, some Cancerians will become a tad too impressionable. So much so, a few might lose contact with plain, ordinary, old-fashioned common sense and go off at a tangent. Any criticism of such actions will not be deemed right or necessary. This could cause a few problems in their romantic life, whether married or single. For the married folk there might be strong disagreements with their in-laws while with the single people the partner is quite likely to just get up and go away.

On 30 March 2025 Neptune enters Aries, the Cancerian subject's tenth house. There will be extremes of behaviour and ability shown by the subjects. If they pursue any of their old ideas from when Neptune was in Pisces there may be difficulties holding on to their jobs and, because of what they might get up to (depending on what they get up to) there could even be a scandal.

If, on the other hand, these people apply themselves to what they do then by their achievements they will become so well-known all manner of good things will come their way. This could include their income, personal status in business and socially a change of address to a better environment. Those in the public eye by virtue of their career might find this part of their life really take off.

Neptune turns retrograde on 4 July 2025 and, a few weeks later re-enters Pisces on 22 October 2025. There won't be much of a change unless the subject tries to go back to the ways he or she used to be and any good will undone. Neptune enters Aries again on 26 January 2026 and will stay there until well after 2030 has passed.

Pluto

As the period under review opens Pluto is in Capricorn and as this is their natural 7th house then it is to be expected that there will be one or two changes in attitude. Recently married folk may seek out new friends, the older the better because these people always get on well those who have more experience of life than they do. Quite a few older relationships could just fade and go by the board; they won't be pursued as actively as before. Cancer folk of all ages and both sexes will have to learn or re-learn from what occurs in these next few years. They may become a tad unpredictable at times because no one, even those near to them will know what might be driving them in their lives. He or she will develop a strong knack for spotting where trouble may lie and, therefore thinks that (he or she) can resolve the problem their way. If illness occurs they must see the correct authority and not allow whatever the weakness is to get of hand.

A streak of selfishness is likely with some getting a little too inconsiderate at times. Just about anything they no longer value is liable to be ended as they develop new friends and associates and that a few power struggles might materialise. Legal matters might also turn up which suggests that a few Cancerians might not like the idea of using professional help and try do-it-yourself tactics. This will only speed up a possible downfall if the issues are serious. During this period marriage is possible and the partner will be a much stronger-willed character than they are. Alternatively or, in some cases as well, a new business partnership is probable.

With all of this in mind please bear in mind that Pluto is in Capricorn until 23 March 2023 when it enters Aquarius.

It will stay in Cancer's eighth house here for just over a year and a lot of good could happen but much depends on how much the subject will want to get along with those around him or her. Trivia may be disregarded while they push themselves into what they consider to be the more serious aspects of life such as their business interests, home and family life and some social activities. When changes do occur, or these people are forced to change their attitude or way of life they will seem to become less serious in their ways. They will have to learn by their mistakes.

Pluto retrogrades back into Capricorn on 11 June 2023 but in some six months or so it swings back again into Aquarius on 21 January 2024. It hardly has time to become settled when it returns to Capricorn on 1 September 2024. Once again, after only a few weeks here it moves back into Aquarius on 19 November 2024 and will remain there for nearly 20 years until 2043.

CHAPTER ELEVEN

Leo

Jupiter

Jupiter is in Aquarius for the first four months or so of 2021. For nearly two years it is not going to be that easy to contend with the planet and the back and forth swing between the first few signs as it settles in to the 2021–2030 period under review. When Jupiter decides to move retrograde it acts rather like a forward moving planet Saturn. It often appears to act as a rather restrictive factor within some of the ideas and plans you may wish to get settled and out of the way.

So, this first but rather short period will serve to influence Leo people about how their democratic inner self ought to come a tad more to the surface. Jupiter in Leo's seventh house and Aquarius to boot will help to make them more open, friendly and approachable than ever before. While a few might take a bit more than they should for granted, most will make themselves almost scrupulously fair in the way they deal with other folk. Nevertheless, cooperation might be a little hard to manage initially. He or she will have to become a lot more prudent than they are used to if they are to succeed.

After 13 May 2021 Jupiter moves on into Pisces and the eighth house of Leo. Married Leo men and women will find their partners more amenable and easier to negotiate with on all sorts of things, especially in their joint financial arrangements. Family monies or those of other people close to you may need your attention. The younger single male and female Leo folk should enjoy both their old and new relationships. One or two of those born toward the end of the sign could become a little difficult to approach.

Jupiter retrogrades back into Aquarius on 28 July 2021 for around five months. The Leo nature should soften slightly but they will have to watch occasional flashes of over-generosity. Marriage or, in these more modern times, co-habitation is possible for some during the summer months.

On 29 December 2021 Jupiter re-enters Pisces. Children will now start to play a larger part in Leo lives. This may be from those already here or, perhaps, for a few who may be awaiting the birth of a newcomer to the family.

On 10 May 2022 Jupiter enters Aries, the ninth house for Leo subjects. Educational pursuits for both themselves and their offspring should become a feature of some importance. This may involve travel, possibly abroad, or just a period (or periods) away from the family home. The health and well-being of all Leo people will be quite good about now which is good news for those involved in any long and or contractual arrangements.

Jupiter retrogrades back into Pisces on 28 October 2022 for a few weeks. This will give those who want to finalise any outstanding business matters a chance to do so. Those who own their own company may well be looking for another small business with a view to either merge or completely take over.

This great planet starts to move forward once and re-enters Aries on 20 December 2022. Something new and quite innovative may be called into play as Leo people go all out to strengthen their hold on their position at work. This will attract a lot of people especially those who matter in other companies. For a few there may be an opportunity to pursue two occupations at the same time, at least for a short while.

On 16 May 2023 Jupiter enters Taurus where it begins a long period of direct motion through the signs and houses. While in Taurus, many ambitions may be realised as promotions or new job offers come their way. Whatever you decide to do, try to choose wisely and carefully. When you do so, make a mental note to not neglect any family matters of any kind for any reason. If you don't do this you could destroy everything you have been working for over the years. Jupiter here suggests that while all may seem well you must not neglect any or all the things with which you may be involved. Keep your hand on the rudder at all times for this not a good time to lose face, position or prestige.

Jupiter begins a transit of Gemini on 25 May 2024. Once it has established itself in the eleventh house of this Air sign both male and female Leo folk will become quite broadminded and much easier to get along with; far approachable than before. The world of communication will open up many avenues for them to consider and the Internet may be one of them. Most of these speculative ventures should prove quite worthwhile in later times.

Jupiter enters Cancer on 9 June 2025. While here the main influence is likely to be for them to begin to create better relationships all round more especially with those who have not always seen eye to eye with their policies. Some of what Leo has considered to be petty restrictions imposed one way or another as to how they work will seem to just fade away. The Leo subject who has become the manager or the boss is going to find themselves feeling rather "out of it". When all else seems to not work listen to your intuition.

On 30 June 2026 Jupiter begins a transit of Leo and all Leo folk will want to feel free to do what they want to do during this period. They will pursue a more physically active time when they can get away from their career responsibilities. They need to hold back on any ego trip where they might display a tad too much self-confidence. They haven't got all the answers (yet) so ease back. Now would be a good time to pay more attention to their partner and family. The boss will be eyeing Leo people for possible changes in the near future.

Virgo receives Jupiter on 26 July 2027 and money matters will matter quite a bit in the coming months. For most of the time there will few problems but Leo folk do occasionally get carried away thinking that they have more than they actually do have. Within the home or socially there could be a tendency to go over the top when celebrating anything. This would be a good time to sit down and work out a few more immediate goals rather than any long-term ambitions.

Jupiter moves on into Libra on 24 August 2028. This will bring more advice and guidance from many sources as you make more friends and more than casual acquaintances in the working arena. There should be an increase in communications with people at work and also within the family especially involving siblings. You are advised to not commit to any new ventures until you have had a real chance to evaluate them.

On 24 September 2029 Jupiter enters Scorpio the Leo fourth house. You must attend to all of your domestic problems promptly, a few of which may have been waiting rather a long while for your attention. Leo people must ensure their home life is safe and secure while they have the chance. Because Leo folk cannot abide being told rather than asked to do things those around them should broach such matters diplomatically.

The last port of call for Jupiter in this period will be Sagittarius and the transit begins on 22 October 2030. Any children or younger people in the family as a whole may turn to you for some advice, assistance or guidance in some way. Single folk will find their love life liable become a tad more spicy than before. You are also likely to become more open and approachable and may even widen your social circle. You must resist any temptation to "stray" no matter how interesting such a situation may appear.

Saturn

Saturn is in Aquarius as 2021 opens and while in the seventh house of Leo, relationships with some of those thought to be friends might be responsible for causing more than just a problem by the way they behave toward you or your position at work. Leo youngsters may have similar problems if still in some form of educational pursuit. Single Leo partners might be helpful but if they feel it might harm their relationship with such people, they might even try to persuade you that you are in the wrong.

Elsewhere, Saturn placed here suggests the possibility of taking on new skills at work.

Saturn enters Pisces on 7 March 2023. For those who have just ended a liaison, romance or even a marriage they might find that actively seeking a new partner might not be that difficult. Saturn here confers intuition and compassion and inclines people to not mix too much. This can often attract others at times. If or when Leo folk might become involved in financial issues they might also find a new person of interest as well. At the end of this relatively short period (for Saturn) Leo might well look back and marvel at his or her changes in the way they now see life.

Saturn moves into Aries on 25 May 2025 and in the ninth house it will try to start to influence people in the way they assess progress of any kind. However, almost five months later Saturn moves back into Pisces on 1 September 2025 for around five months or so. The best advice is to go with the sway of things and hold your peace. It will only be for a few months and your day-to-day affairs won't alter that much.

On 14 February 2026 Saturn re-enters Aries. This will create a lot of self-willed actions on your part and any success that you do have will be largely through your own efforts because other folk will not have been that helpful. They won't oppose you so much as just not get involved – but that shouldn't worry Leo people at all. Travel generally should be beneficial and some of your long-term financial arrangements may come to fruition. Saturn may be in fall here but just about everything should be going your way.

On 13 April 2028 Saturn will begin a transit of Taurus. Now Leo people can reap the rewards of a lot of hard work and even behind-the-scenes preparatory activities should also come into being for them. Whatever you do get up to do remember that you have a personal life that will need your attention if you spend too much time on work or other affairs. Married people will suffer the most here because most single folk have a better knack of correcting anything that isn't quite up to scratch. Obstinacy or stubbornness won't go down too well but the proper way of doing things the right way will.

On 1 June 2030 Saturn edges into Gemini. Most Leo folk will work better if they involve themselves in team or group activities. This is no time to try and go-it-alone, it just won't work. The older Leo person will be more successful during this transit than the younger man or woman. This spell coincides with the hopes and wishes that the Leo character has always cherished either publicly or privately. It might not be a good idea to actually start anything completely new (businesswise) around now but just about anything else in your personal life should go the way you hope. For some of the younger folk a career in some form of educational pursuit might be worthwhile.

Uranus

As the period under review opens Uranus is in Taurus and will remain there for the next five years. While many Leo people love change they are probably not going be that taken with might happen around now. Change is more than probable but precisely what will be up to you. Managers and the overall bosses can seem to be a hard-headed lot at times. You have to make up your mind to stay with what you know (and whom) or go to another organisation about which you know little but in a position to wield your authority your way.

On 7 July 2025 Uranus moves into Gemini. Once in the eleventh house of Leo you will begin to see that to get along with others you are going have to change, to become more approachable along with a little of your old ways and bit more of the new – for you at any rate. There are going to be changes so you must either work with them or find yourself left behind in more ways than one. Where you might have become bored easily there may well be little time for such things as time moves on.

Just as you start to get used to the idea of what is happening Uranus retreats back into Taurus on 8 November 2025. This will be a short stay of some six months or so when the planet will be retrograde most of the time until it turns direct again on 3 Feb 2026. When retrograde, Uranus in the Leonian tenth house will seem to block one or two issues but there won't be that much time for this to happen because On 26 April 2026 Uranus moves on again into Gemini where it will remain until 2032.

Neptune

As the period under review opens up Neptune will be in Pisces until 2025. For the next ten years Neptune will be in either Pisces or Aries.

While in Pisces, Neptune will begin to influence the way you operate in general. You will start to become more practical in the way you deal with everything which, hopefully, will include financial matters of all kinds. Money, perhaps that of others or joint arrangements will need astute handling for much of what will be required. Future issues rather than what may be wanted today are likely to be the keynote here so be willing to listen and take advice. If you have the slightest doubt about anything seek professional advice.

On 30 March 2025 Neptune enters Aries, the ninth house of Leo. This rather slow moving planet will hardly have time to do anything of any consequence when it turns retrograde on 4 July 2025 and re-enters Pisces on 22 October 2025. Just a few weeks later Neptune moves back again into Aries again on 26 January 2026 and will stay there until well after 2030 has passed.

Quite a few subtle changes are going to occur in the next four years some of which you will fight initially. Once you accept a few new ideas, you will soon settle down and move with the times and a lot more of the new faces around you.

Pluto

As the period under review opens Pluto is in Capricorn and on 23 March 2023 Pluto enters Aquarius. and for the whole of the ten years under review please take note that Pluto only moves back and forth between these two signs for the whole period.

Pluto in Capricorn is not the best of places for this planet because it will influence a lot of problems for individuals as well as organisations and one or two countries as well. However, for Leo people take note that you can only do so much at a time. Where before you may have really spread your wings and worked all hours to achieve the aim of whatever it was you were working on this time you will have to stop and re-think things through. The best answer is to try to delegate. This may not go down too well but it is one of many changes that are going to come about. If you continue as you are poor health is likely – stop worrying about telling people what to do and bend with the wind a lot more.

Some may actually be given the opportunity to change their job altogether either within the company you are presently with or you might change employers altogether.

Aquarius receives Pluto on 23 March 2023, the seventh house for Leo subjects. New technology and fresh ideas will go down well and you may dream up quite a few around now. Leo people in close personal relationships could have their work cut out here. They will have to pay more attention to their partners whether they are married or single. These companions are not being difficult; they just want the attention they think is their due. While this is taking a little while to sink in Pluto edges back into Capricorn again just a few weeks or so later.

So, on 11 June 2023 Pluto retrogrades back into Capricorn and for around six months and starts to wield its old ideas on Leo folk again. The planet has a way of breaking down old habits, ideas and plans and then allows you to re-think this or that because the air is somewhat clearer as a result.

By the time that realisation is upon you it moves direct again and on 21 January 2024 Pluto edges forward into Aquarius again. Things now start to get a tad hairy for a lot of people. These changes of direction are not quite its usual routine but that doesn't help at all, because its influence is still there. Bear in mind what was said before and add that you are going to have to deal with a few new faces, quite a few old ones and some of your more open or up-front enemies. These may include one or two of your working colleagues who just don't like the way you work or, perhaps, the way you go about things.

Once again and after some seven months or so Pluto returns to Capricorn on 1 September 2024. This is liable to ease back on some of the pressures. It should also give you more time to sit down to re-plan and re-think a few of your various strategies. There may be a few legal wrangles that you have not had time to think through as much as you should have done. Advertising may be one of the areas needing your attention.

Hardly seven weeks have passed when Pluto moves back into Aquarius again on 19 November 2024 to stay until 2043. You now have a lot longer to consider the path or paths you should follow to achieve your ambitions.

CHAPTER TWELVE

Virgo

Jupiter

Jupiter is in Aquarius as 2021 opens and for something like two years or so, it is going to be rather a difficult job trying to keep up with it. It will spend a lot of time moving back and forth between the first few signs while it settles in for the period under review. Jupiter retrograde tends to influence matters, rather like a forward moving Saturn. On more than a few occasions, it seems to act more like a restrictive element with some of the wishes of some of the Virgo subjects. Just be aware as we get things under way.

Thus, Jupiter is in Aquarius as 2021 opens, the sixth house for Virgo. These people may expect a reasonably good period while the planet holds sway here. It should start a fairly beneficial time for most Virgo subjects. With the probable rise of an increased spell of self-confidence, there may be more than one attempt to make changes in the working arena. This should be rejected because this is not a good time for any serious alteration to the lifestyle. While travel for business purposes may attract, try to keep such activities to a minimum.

When Jupiter enters Pisces on 13 May 2021 the prospects for marriage or longer lasting liaisons for other single Virgos looks quite promising. Actual marriage may not occur this time round, for Jupiter is only here for about six weeks or so before it retrogrades back into Aquarius again on 28 July 2021. Jupiter's

VIRGO

switching about between these two signs will help Virgos get their acts together. It isn't usual for these subjects to be seen to be generous but there is a chance of over-doing it as they try to re-arrange their affairs with more concrete or practical moves. They will need the help of other folk because this is their way of doing things.

On 29 December 2021 Jupiter moves forward once more and enters Pisces again, but this time Virgo folk will be ready for the fray. In the event of being unable to handle certain issues that may occur, don't hesitate to call in a professional in that field. It is never a good time to try to resolve such things yourself – you are not trained.

Jupiter pushes on into Aries on May 10 2022 but will only be there for about four months. Financial matters of some kind will become prominent; an inheritance of some kind or a bond may mature. For others, there may be a chance of joining forces perhaps in a business matter of some kind.

On 28 October 2022 Jupiter retrogrades back into Pisces for a few weeks and for some the chance of letting things slide or becoming a tad unreliable is possible. Virgo people are either super-efficient when they put their minds to it or, and it does happen, they can turn into complete slobs. Once Jupiter turns direct again, those Virgo people who did let go will soon get their act together again. Things will speed up in general and Jupiter will re-enter Aries on 20 December 2022, where it will stay for about six months.

On 16 May 2023 Jupiter enters Taurus and will be there for a year. This will be a year of expansion in many ways; money, possessions and, quite possibly, around the waist as well. Look after yourself because the ninth house of Virgo isn't always that benevolent if or when things are allowed to get out of control. You may have to deal with people from abroad or perhaps actually travel there. This could be thought of as silly advice for a Virgo perhaps but don't assume anything, make sure you know all there is to know. Keep an open mind at all times when dealing with colleagues.

On 25 May 2024 Jupiter edges into Gemini to stay for a shade over a year. This is your tenth house and the accent will be on career issues mostly. Promotion, a transfer or being asked to head up something new and or different is likely. Don't be afraid to say no should you feel so inclined; be more true to yourself rather than your pocket or status. In some cases this might even be a wise move. It might be a little on the useful side to dabble a little less than usual in spite of what you learn. At some time in this period the world of communication in all its forms world may attract.

Cancer will welcome Jupiter as it begins to transit your eleventh house on 9 June 2025. This planet is in exaltation in this sign and much should go your way for yet another period. However, there are one of two things you should be aware of or should avoid. Friends and associates will help you become more settled. Try to avoid becoming self-centred and or selfish. If you should become involved in a gambling streak, ease back as soon as possible or don't get mixed up with the idea in the first place.

The great planet begins its journey through Leo on 30 June 2026. Another good year in which you will be free to pursue all sorts of activities and may even be encouraged by one or two more senior people at work. Incidents from the past should be put right about now and old friends who were involved then will become closer as a result. A strongly creative and self-confident time will now be in evidence.

On 26 July 2027 Jupiter enters your own sign of Virgo. Close personal relationships will become even more so with many single Virgo folk positively relishing their time with new friends and partners. This will eventually become a quite prosperous period for most Virgo people but they must take care not to become too extravagant. There is a danger of becoming overly concerned with detail often always wanting time to think things through before deciding on this or that. Up to a point, that is very good, but this year it shouldn't be necessary.

On 24 August 2028 Jupiter moves into Libra. Once the influence of Jupiter gets to work in your second house financial of arrangements most money matters may be finalised or begun as you see fit. You might become a tad too reliant on other folk or just the opposite and become a shade too independent. Either way, ease back if either of these ways start to develop. You ought to seriously consider the future and think of your financial retirement arrangements.

Jupiter enters Scorpio on 24 September 2029. Pat attention to what you say and to whom you say it. When writing letters or even emails check them carefully so that no one can throw them back at you while trying to "have a go" at the same time. You will become more and more in demand as new contacts, business colleagues, associates and friends come on to the scene – but not all will be on your side and this you may not find out until it is too late.

Jupiter moves on into Sagittarius on 22 October 2030. Family members, siblings or other immediate family members may turn to you for help and guidance. This also a time to ensure that all family and domestic arrangements are in order because there is an outside chance you may be considering the possibility of moving house.

Saturn

Saturn is in Aquarius as 2021 opens. This planet in the sixth house suggests Virgo people probably won't achieve very much as these two years progress, for this is when much of the preparation for such aims are best carried out. So, those of you with ambitions in any direction should start to pave your way about now. There is an outside chance of ills and pains that could interfere with any programme you set in motion. Be careful not to upset co-workers (you can be a tad too demanding at times) and try to take any delays in your stride.

Saturn enters Pisces on 7 March 2023 the seventh house of partnerships of all kinds. Planets here also show how the subject views and collaborates with his or her associates at any level in business or in private. The more people try to use you and your talents, the less you will want to get along with them. Unfortunately, this attitude may spread to other folk. While you are in this stage, do remember to pay plenty of attention to your partner or things could turn nasty, perhaps more so for the married couples. All this may take you away from your business aims. The tensions will rise if anything really gets out of hand.

Saturn moves into Aries on 25 May 2025. This could be a rather difficult three months or so before Saturn retrogrades back into Pisces later in the year. Money may become tight, and people who owe you money may not (or won't be able to) pay you back. Elsewhere money may also prove to be just as hard to come by. Borrowing could prove awkward as well, so it would be best to keep a very tight hold on your financial matters as well as any other matters entrusted to you.

On 1 September 2025 Saturn retrogrades back into Pisces until mid-February 2026. Once again, not the happiest of times perhaps for as long as you keep a keen eye on everything under your personal control.

Saturn move back into Aries on 14 February 2026. Any areas where you wield responsibility could come under some sort of pressure. The partner's affairs may need your expert way of dealing with such things. It is remotely possible that a legacy may appear but because of what it is, it may take more time than you care for to actually become yours. This will not be an easy period but as long as you see to things as they occur you will survive and gain much in experience as well.

On 13 April 2028 Saturn enters Taurus. Saturn here will measure how well you cope with ninth house affairs and the way in which you manage your affairs. As long as you accept that there will always be a few limitations with everyday life issues, this will be a good period. You should be able to slowly but steadily move ahead with your aims and ambitions. Some extra travel is likely. This will be a good time to push ahead with all or any or long-term aims.

On 1 June 2030 Saturn will edge into Gemini, the tenth house for Virgo subjects. You ought to be able to reap at least some of the rewards for all your efforts. You may become a shade too set in your ways at times so play things with care. Apart from a possible upward move your personal reputation, social and (local) public standing will be to your benefit.

Uranus

As the period under review opens Uranus is in Taurus for the next five years. For the rest of the ten years under review the planet swings back and forth between Taurus and Gemini.

While in Taurus Uranus tends to influence Virgo folk to show their rather clever and most practical attitude to life in general in both business and the private world. Unfortunately, it also creates a stubborn streak that does sometimes get out of control. If you become involved in travel matters or the communication world change tack and open up to show just how flexible you can be. Financially, you can show the world what a whizz-kid really can do when he or she tries. Money begets money as a rule but resist the urge to gamble at any level. If you get hooked you are liable to lose everything. Be ready to accept new ideas, it doesn't matter from whom, because it will open up entirely new vistas for some.

On 7 July 2025 Uranus moves into Gemini and while for just a few weeks this time the planet will incline you to be a rather more strong-willed and determined character. You will begin to notice that those around you in your business arena may try to repress some of your ideas but, unfortunately, and before you can do much about it, Uranus swings back in to Taurus on 8 November 2025.

This will be a stay of about six months and the planet stays retrograde most of the time until it turns direct again on 3 Feb 2026. When retrograde, Uranus in your ninth house will either curb your enthusiasm or it will allow it full rein. You must tread a very careful path between these two extremes. It won't be for long because on 26 April 2026 Uranus moves on again into Gemini where it will remain until well after the 2030. It would be a good idea to work more in the background and only come out to adjust here and there to put things back on track again. There will be opportunities to completely change your career direction, to take a promotion or a transfer as you so wish. You may even decide not to do anything and stay as you are.

Neptune

As 2021 opens Neptune is in Pisces which is the seventh house for Virgo subjects. For the next four years or so all relationships will become quite important but more especially the close, one-to-one types whether they are in your personal, social or business life. Married couples should grow closer to each other while single folk will make the most of opportunity as it comes their way. Socially, people with whom you deal regularly close or otherwise and business colleagues will all look to you for advice and guidance as such things occur. Those Virgo folk who feel they might do better in a partnership should think twice and weigh up all the pro's and con's very carefully for this is not that good an idea at present. Work and play with whom you like but in really serious matters take care.

Some of you will turn to the arts, music or the theatre perhaps and this could lead to more exciting things later. Elsewhere you might want to ease back altogether and just enjoy life as it comes. However, the pursuit of pleasure could become a tad too easy to get used to. Try not to slip back too far.

On 30 March 2025 Neptune enters Aries but it will hardly have time to settle and begin to influence anything because about six months later it turns retrograde on 4 July 2025 and re-enters Pisces on 22 October 2025. It will be there for about twelve weeks or so and re-enter Aries again on 26 January 2026 to remain there until long after 2030 has passed.

Neptune in Aries tends to make people a tad too sensitive for their own good and hint of selfishness can creep in. Old ideals or aims may come back to either haunt or aid some folk. It is also possible that any joint arrangement of a financial nature may have to be attended to during this period. Decisions made around now could have far-reaching effects so think, and think long and hard before making any definite moves. You may be asked to look after the affairs of an older relative or of a very close friend.

Pluto

As this period opens Pluto is in Capricorn and for the next ten years it will move back and forth between Capricorn and Aquarius. While in Capricorn, its influence will be felt mostly in your working arena but it will also incline you to the pursuit of pleasure in more ways than one. Offspring or any younger element in your family life may have to look to you for help and assistance in some way. These requests must not be delayed or ignored. You could risk losing their respect and admiration and they could just simply cut you out of their lives altogether.

Outdoor activities may attract and not only in the realms of sport. At the very least this might be gardening in some way or, possibly, something to do with country pursuits perhaps. This might require you to attend evening classes for a while and could be connected to your working life so that you can add a little more experience to the career as well following up on something new that you come to like.

A word of warning is now offered. Whether married or single quite a few Virgo folk could encounter an opportunity for very close relationships to happen. The excitement of straying is one thing but think of what might happen if your partner found out. For single folk such things are part and parcel of life anyway but married couples have, or should have more love and respect for their partner unless, of course, things are at such a point whatever the partner does in his or her own time is their business.

On 23 March 2023 Pluto enters Aquarius for barely three months. In this sign Virgo people should always keep an eye on their work and their health for the one may be dependent on the other. Because anything new or different challenges the mind people tend to become almost obsessed while they pursue what has attracted them. Often, this leads to health problems for the individual fails to get enough rest and relaxation. There will even be a few who will work all night at times, if given the opportunity. On top of this, while they take part in their leisure activities they can become so caught up with this new outlook on life they forget their obligations. So, the reverse can happen and, in their haste to catch up elsewhere the health of Virgo people can suffer this way.

Pluto retrogrades back into Capricorn on 11 June 2023 to stay for about six months and then on 21 January 2024 Pluto edges forward to re-enter Aquarius again. Three months or so after this, the planet returns once again to move back into Capricorn on 1 September 2024. It really has little to start to influence anything when on 19 October 2024 Pluto moves forward to enter Aquarius again on 19 November 2024. It will stay here in the sixth house of Virgo until 2043.

CHAPTER THIRTEEN

Libra

Jupiter

For the first year or so, Jupiter will move back and forth through Aquarius and Pisces, hardly stopping for very long in either sign. So, for this period Jupiter is not going to be easy to assess for whatever influence it may or should produce. When Jupiter acts like this and turns retrograde, its action becomes rather similar to that of the forward moving planet Saturn. There will be occasions when it may become a rather restrictive factor dependent on where it is. When it does move retrograde, Librans may have to re-think and re-direct some of their plans and aims that they may want to get under way. In some cases, they may have to put a hold on everything.

At the beginning of this period Jupiter passes into Aquarius and is there the first four months or so of 2021. Libra people should feel that their social life has at long last got under way and in no uncertain manner. Their character and personality will be very much appreciated in many walks of life. An opportunity for them to further their personal life may come about. Jupiter in Aquarius in the fifth house offers the chance to meet and have a serious relationship with someone from abroad, a different background or age group. This is a time when friendship can turn to love. Married couples who have had trouble in trying to conceive could hear good news.

Jupiter enters Pisces on 13 May 2021 which is when career and employment will come to the fore. However, they really should look at the small print when change is mooted by either the boss or from elsewhere. One or two might slip up and let things slide, which will not be at all helpful. Others may feel they need to get involved in something completely different. In the middle of June, the planet turns retrograde and Librans are likely to feel the pressure in that they cannot seem to get anything off the ground no matter how hard they may have worked to do so.

Jupiter moves back into Aquarius on 28 July 2021 where it will stay for about five months or so but it will remain retrograde until mid-October. As it starts to move forward, all Librans will feel the urge to push their ideas and plans one last time when all should suddenly go well for them.

The great planet quickly moves into Pisces once more on 29 December 2021. For the short time it is here, Librans must look after welfare of their offspring or any member of the younger element of their family. This will bring about a short time for all Libra subjects to watch their budget. All joint family monies ought to be entrusted to the partner for they should be in a better position to handle such things.

Libra people can be a shade over-generous at times and this would help to avoid a possible case of "the best laid plans of mice and men".

On 10 May 2022 Jupiter enters Aries, the Libran seventh house; this will emphasise health and work issues. One or two people may take on two jobs, perhaps for just a short period to either earn extra cash or to follow up something that has intrigued them for some time. If this should happen, they are advised to watch their health. Failure to take adequate rest and relaxation or eat properly can play havoc with Libra subjects, who are not the healthiest people in the zodiac. On the other hand there are one or two who will put on weight because their diet.

On 28 October 2022 Jupiter moves retrograde and returns into Pisces once more for seven weeks or so. It hardly has time to significantly influence anything when it re-enters Aries on 20 December 2022 to stay for five months. Librans are reminded of what was written earlier about this planet in their seventh house.

In the event of any possible legal problem you are advised to seek professional help. Do-it-yourself activities in this field will only lead to more trouble.

Jupiter moves into Taurus on 16 May 2023. Once in the eighth house, Libra subjects will find that there are a lot of people who want them to form a partnership or become a closer friend/ colleague or ally in a new venture or undertaking which should appeal. Librans will also start to reap a few of the rewards due because of their hard work or clever investment abilities much earlier in previous years. Anyone who owes money or who used their services for their own benefit will now seek to not only repay them but also to ensure they are introduced to the right people in the right circles. Married Librans will have to work much closer with their partner to keep all domestic issues and the home in good working order.

A year later, Jupiter enters Gemini on 25 May 2023. This will have the mind working overtime and you will become rather busy in this area. Gemini helps the mind to flourish in this manner and a natural curiosity will help keep the mind fairly versatile. You may well become a tad more broad-minded along with a ready wit. The world of communication will open up to you as you begin to explore this field of endeavour. Travel overseas or to a place or places presently unknown to you perhaps for business purposes could occur around this period.

On 9 June 2025 Jupiter begins a transit of Cancer. This planet in the tenth house of Libra suggests the career and work matters will become even more important to you. One of your special gifts is that of negotiation and the people for whom you work may appoint you on to a panel that deals with such things. In a smaller concern this art will be admired by all and sundry – especially the boss. Promotion is a possibility around now or a transfer or a change of job altogether which will introduce you to many new acquaintances at all levels. All this activity might create a few problems within the family and domestic area. Stress or such tension is not good and you may experience a possible break-up, temporary or permanent. This is not a time to change the address.

Jupiter enters Leo on 30 June 2026. Beware the possibility of an "eternal triangle" liaison which will create quite a fall from grace. Whether single or married you should avoid this type of thing like the plague. Libra people know how to keep a secret but more or less anybody with whom they associate cannot. Take care; try to control your rather over-worked vanity streak. Elsewhere, you should become quite popular within the social circles you tend to frequent.

Jupiter moves into Virgo on 26 July 2027 and this is not the best place for it to be for any length of time. If you take on too much, try to trust and delegate some of this work to others who know what to do – if you let them. Managers and employers may be watching looking to see who they can promote, if not now, later perhaps. This will be a reasonable period as long as you don't rush into anything at work or in the domestic area.

The planet starts a transit of Libra on 24 August 2028. With this in your first house there ought to be no stopping you from doing whatever you want to do. Health and wealth should be good except that self-indulgence will tend to stretch the waistline somewhat. While much will depend upon your attitude as to whether money and position will come your way readily, an approachable and constructive attitude will go a long way in achieving even more.

Jupiter will start its journey through Scorpio on 24 September 2029. Just about everything regarding your overall income should flourish significantly – even your joint arrangements. There could even be a win of some kind coming your way. Personal possessions and status will become important. You will become shrewd, aggressive and quite determined; your head for business will be quite successful.

On 22 October 2030 Jupiter will pass into Sagittarius. Your social life should broaden while relationships with siblings and other close family members should improve. Libra folk may enrol themselves into some form of training study in their spare time. Outdoor pursuits of all kinds will attract. If it is sport, it probably won't be something like direct competition – it will be more of a solo effort either as a part of a team or on your own. If not sport, then it may be something to do with animals in some way.

Saturn

Saturn is in Aquarius as 2021 opens and between now and 2025 Saturn will pass in and out of Pisces and Aquarius. While in Aquarius this planet tends show its influence by teaching you more about yourself than you know. It helps you understand life but it also tends to make you work a lot harder at what you do. This will help to set the success level for you to reach and maintain. Socially, life will improve but it will be mainly to do with your career aspirations. However good you become socially, many younger single folk may shy away from any new close relationships.

Saturn enters Pisces on 7 March 2023. Libra folk should exercise great discretion in the way they work and or play with associates, business colleagues and even their employers. You will become more serious and even a little reserved at times but this will be because of your work which will come first. This is not a good time to gamble in any way for you will be unsuccessful. While at work make sure of the details – don't take chances.

Saturn begins a transit of Aries on 25 May 2025. This is not the time to scatter your efforts or energies. You are sufficiently resourceful to mind your "P's and Q's" at such a time and will even become a trifle self-willed. This may well create a feeling that you have a lack of consideration for those around you. If this attitude is taken too far, domestic differences could arise that you may not be able to resolve. A rather serious period is envisaged here. Initially, only some of these changes may start to happen, if at all, as this planet will only be here for about four months or so.

On 1 September 2025 Saturn retrogrades back into Pisces and will stay there for almost six months. After this, Saturn will move forward again and re-enter Aries on 14 February 2026. It will stay in the Libran sixth house for two years.

Then, on 13 April 2028 Saturn begins to pass through Taurus. Libran folk will become a tad obstinate and rather stubborn at times. This will start because of their commitment to their work. One or two may change their jobs during this period. Relationships and close partnerships are likely and marriage may even occur. Equally, some of these situations may suffer a break-up. The younger single Librans will certainly enjoy this period. Expect a few emotional ups and downs.

On 1 June 2030 Saturn edges into Gemini. The ninth house for Libra brings a better understanding of life, yourself and your overall attitude. Many people will have reached the top of their profession or will have got as far as they can. Saturn here implies more travel than usual which may be connected with their work. Some may lean toward teaching or some form of instruction work. However, the end of the period under review is only six months away and any influence may not have got fully under way by then.

Uranus

Uranus is in Taurus from January 2021 for the next five years. It promises to be quite a stirring time for most Librans in general but at the same time, there are going to be one or two moments when you may regret an action you may have taken. Old ideas, ways and means may begin to attract more and this will exercise the mind quite a bit. There will be a chance for a rather unusual and exciting relationship along lines you may not have experienced before. Married Librans will have cause to be very sorry should this become public knowledge while the single folk will revel in it.

Joint financial arrangements are likely to need a firm hand and there is a chance of an inheritance. Business partnerships should flourish. Those who owe money or who are owed money will find this a period of fluctuation in that some will pay up promptly while others will seek a longer term before they pay.

On 7 July 2025 Uranus moves into Gemini. This will spark off a few changes in both the private and business lives of many

Libran subjects. Many will be attracted to all sorts of new ways of doing things, new thinking and the new challenges that will go with this. Flexibility will be a major necessity – a natural attribute for a Libran. However, Uranus will only be in this position for around four months so not a great deal will actually get under way.

Uranus retreats back into Taurus on 8 November 2025 to stay for around four months or so. Some of the old ways may surface but the planet will remain retrograde until it turns direct on 3 Feb 2026. Retrograde Uranus in the eighth house it will take off some of the pressures but in just a few weeks it moves on again into Gemini on 26 April 2026 and will stay there until 2030 has passed.

Neptune

For the next ten years Neptune will be in either Pisces or Aries but from 1 January 2021 it will be in Pisces for just over four years. While here the planet tends to influence work interests and health and these two can become rather dependent on each other. The harder you work the more chance of you neglecting your health with insufficient rest and or a poor diet. Spare time activities may be taken up with a fascination for the unknown or with subjects like astrology or vegetarianism perhaps. Check with a local astrologer for any OOB planets around now. The welfare of other folk might also take up some of your time. Beware of upsetting your immediate manager or employer by such actions or by being a tad too outspoken re business matters.

On 30 March 2025 Neptune will begin to transit Aries and will stay there for around six month or so. Your imagination will start to be a lot more active than it ever has been and there will be a hint of some unorthodoxy in the way you express yourself. Some conventions may be consigned to wherever while you assume a different attitude to many things.

Neptune turns retrograde on 4 July 2025 and re-enters Pisces on 22 October 2025. Neptune cannot work much influence at such a speed, for it is only here for about three months then it moves into Aries again on 26 January 2026 and will stay there until well after 2030 has passed.

Pluto

As the period under review opens Pluto is in Capricorn. For the next two years or so, Librans will become quite conscious of and active in their domestic arrangements. Work related issues will not be allowed to interfere here at all and their home really will become their castle. Any attempt, however small will get a very firm "no". In such matters, Librans will be quite firm and even dictatorial. There may be a change of address on the cards for some. The younger element will become a lot closer to their parents. These changes are consistent with the way Pluto acts in Capricorn.

On 23 March 2023 Pluto enters Aquarius but is hardly here for more than a few weeks, which really gives it far too little time to get any influence under way.

Pluto retrogrades back into Capricorn on 11 June 2023 and for some six months or so will not be able to take up where it left off because it remains retrograde until 12 October 2023. If you are going to change your address however, it might well be in this period. When it does turn direct again some, not all, of what I described earlier may start up again.

On 21 January 2024 Pluto edges back into Aquarius again. The next eight months or so are likely to see Libran people set much store by their relationships of all kinds in their business, social and private lives. Another feature that can occur will be that the usual open-minded Librans could start to search for other things or activities to keep them occupied. Young people and their fields of interest may attract here.

Married couples will almost certainly be called on to look into what their own offspring might need or decide or decree what educational pursuits they ought to or should follow. Some Librans may even change tack altogether and become interested or active in the entertainment world. They might actually enjoy working in the background of their local theatre for example.

Pluto once again returns into Capricorn 1 September 2024 for barely six weeks. This is no time at all even for such a strong planet like Pluto to start to influence anything.

Pluto re-enters Aquarius on 19 November 2024 where it will remain until 2043. Now the planet has all the time in the world to start influencing what it wants its way. As a rule, Pluto tends to break down existing arrangements where it deems change is necessary and then help re-build it all again. Pluto in Aquarius will also make Libra people take up a stronger interest in science and technology. This might be anything from the ordinary computer world to the highly technical mobile phone and tablet industry partly because these people have always had an active interest in getting along and communicating with others. Also, remember, Librans have a gift for mediation and negotiation and so, therefore, such a new (?) interest would be so useful.

CHAPTER FOURTEEN

Scorpio

Jupiter

It will be a little difficult to accurately forecast in any detail what or how Jupiter is going to influence anything in the first two years or so because it hardly stays still in one place for any reasonable time as it prowls in and out of Aquarius, Pisces and Aries. But, once it does get going things will be better all round. Jupiter retrograde tends to act rather like a forward motion Saturn and can seem a tad restrictive at times.

So, Jupiter starts 2021 in Aquarius for the first four months or so. While here in Scorpio's fourth house its influence will be mostly on their domestic affairs. A change of address or a new purchase along similar lines may be under consideration, not an actual move – yet. Scorpio subjects will tend to be a little erratic in their overall approach and rather intense. If an interest in politics begins to grow, you would do well to remember that you would operate best on the outer edges rather than become a full blown local or national representative. Additionally, you appear to carry the weight and authority to become a representative in union work. Your skills in the way you manage and mediate are quite respected.

Jupiter moves into Pisces on 13 May 2021 for a very short period when it turns retrograde and moves back into Aquarius again for five months. It really has very little time, if any at all, to exert any influence when it behaves in this fashion.

On 28 July 2021 we find Jupiter in Aquarius again where we will try to pick up the pieces from a little earlier. Try to plan your daily grind so that you won't be over-busy one day with very little to do the next. Too much action at any one time will not be good for your health, for the first thing you are likely to neglect is your diet. Any possible temporary financial embarrassment might be alleviated by either set of parents.

Jupiter heads back into Pisces again on 29 December 2021. Single Scorpio folk of either sex will find this a rather romantic period. When one is young suitors seem to come and go but around now many of these young people will find this to be a more serious time for their affections. Married couples are more likely to strengthen their ties. However, there is a risk of straying and a short-lived "eternal triangle" affair could begin. There is an ability to teach and or instruct so, should the opportunity open up with your company for such a position if you should apply for the chances are you would be successful. Curiously, the willingness to learn also sits strong. You could enrol in an evening school class for what has always held something for you.

On 10 May 2022 Jupiter enters Aries for around five months. In the Scorpio sixth house Jupiter tends to influence just about all aspects of career issues but in a few cases it may be at the cost of neglecting some of the domestic arrangements. This will create problems Scorpio folk can ill-afford at this time. If any of the argument is because they are suggesting holding down two jobs, even for a little while, the partner will try to wipe the floor with them. At this juncture, it would be wise to remind you to "neither a lender nor borrower be". Working at or from home is definitely not on.

Jupiter re-enters Pisces once more on 28 October 2022 for a few weeks, just long enough to re-kindle on or two old passions perhaps.

Then, on 20 December 2022 the great planet re-enters Aries once again for yet another six month stay. For some any change of career might bring them into the one of medical fields, social welfare or even catering perhaps. These are ideal places for them to really shine either as an employer or employee. Scorpio people have an intense dislike of feeling hemmed in or restricted in any way. Jupiter here will lend you strength to oppose any attempt at trying to hold you back unnecessarily. A sense of humour properly applied will keep you out of most scrapes but do take care.

On 16 May 2023 Jupiter finally moves properly direct again and enters Taurus. Those who are in a position where they entrust others to look after their financial affairs should check up on the person or persons involved. This does not imply fraud but just possible out and out plain carelessness. If they can find people to co-operate with them in the way they would prefer then all well and good. However, Scorpio can be inclined to trust a tad too much in this area as well. Therefore, they would do well to resist indulgence and act more prudently.

From 25 May 2024 Jupiter begins to pass through Gemini. A few Scorpio people may turn to studying mystical or occult reading or even look to religious matters in some cases. Personal finances or those belonging to others who have asked you to look after their assets may become prominent and will need your special attention. There is a chance of an inheritance in this period and money may come in via a small gambling win, even if it is just the Lottery. Some of you may begin to study up on the art and science of communication on computers, mobile phones or tablets. There will be a need to keep the mind open and receptive.

Jupiter enters Cancer on 9 June 2025, which is helpful because the ninth house of Scorpio has always been considered beneficial. Despite how good you are or what others might think of your ability in business, this and similar matters will develop. Travel may also be in the air probably related to your career interests because it wouldn't be like you to just want go on holiday – you would want to do other things as well. An interest in work on the land could develop.

Jupiter begins to pass through Leo on 30 June 2026. Watch out for the way you might seem to start to behave for there is a chance of becoming arrogant, over-bearing and positively dislikeable in some quarters. In these coming months, this is the last thing you will want. People in the public eye can ill-afford this happening to them so be warned. Elsewhere, just about everything is all set for an upswing in your job and career matters, part of which may to do with training. People from overseas may begin to become an influence in your work, which could lead to even better things in due course and that might include travel abroad.

On 26 July 2027 Jupiter edges into Virgo your eleventh house. The future will begin to take shape in your mind as well as physically – but only up to a point. You can see what you want and you will be happy to plan ahead for such things. Friends and associates from your social circles will be of great help with their influence in certain places. However, within the scope of your employment arena very little seems to be on offer as the new Jupiter period opens. It will be up to you to pull your socks up and work hard for what you want.

When Jupiter enters Libra on 24 August 2028 quite a few changes, some a tad subtle at first will start to make your life a lot easier. Those who work more in the background are more likely to notice this. Where you thought you were missing out in career issues, managers and employers have been assessing your worth for later. Whatever is offered should be accepted. Any changes you feel might be helpful can always be negotiated later.

The great planet Jupiter moves into your own sign on 24 September 2029. The world should be your oyster, that is, unless you are careless and put a foot wrong. This should prove to be a period of expansion for your personal financial arrangements. Family life and social affairs should expand. Do be careful not to neglect any health matters that could come about if you over do the working side of life.

Saturn begins its sojourn in Sagittarius on 22 October 2030 but in the nine weeks or so that is left of the year, very little will start happen. However, you will want to increase your possessions and ensure you have sufficient resources to keep up such a momentum.

Saturn

Saturn is in Aquarius as 2021 opens which is the Scorpio fourth house. The older person may be asked or will have to take charge of a youngster to guide them on their way as they grow and mature. This could be a shade irksome, especially if there any upsets within the domestic scene. You are going to have to take a step back to assess what you are like and what you want from life. If nothing else you will become quite practical in many ways.

On March 27 2023 Saturn enters Pisces. Whatever else you do you are going to have to work harder to just maintain the status quo but despite this the rewards will be well worth the effort. Any natural shyness won't help your cause so get out there and let the world know where and who you are. While close attachments may not be for you, many of your friends seem to be well placed to help you through this rather stark time.

Saturn moves on into Aries on 25 May 2025 and although here for just a short while this planet can help to develop your plans but a tad slower than you might wish. Take care not to upset any of your work colleagues or other associates. Promotion is in the air and if you are aware of this, then so are they.

On 1 September 2025 Saturn retrogrades back into Pisces, which we have already suggested could produce a few difficulties for Scorpions. Saturn turns direct on again on 2 October when things should ease quite a bit.

Saturn returns to Aries on 14 February 2026. Your capacity for detail along with your steady hand on the tiller will eventually prove profitable but don't push too hard in any direction. This is not a good time to upset anyone at any level in the work arena.

Just over two years later on 13 April 2028, Saturn enters Taurus, your seventh house. For just over two years or so, how you get along with people at home, socially or at work will have a bearing on the level of any success that should come your way. Saturn here is not too keen on any imbalance of approach by anyone to anyone. Being stubborn won't help here, try to relax more and let others come to you.

On 1 June 2030 Saturn edges into Gemini and you will have to work to maintain a well ordered and disciplined approach to all and sundry. The next six months could be quite a testing time through to the end of this period under review. Any joint financial arrangements look like being quite promising and should help you to plan more effectively for your future.

Uranus

As the period under review opens Uranus is in Taurus for the next five years. There may well be a strong desire to get away from it all, to be more independent and in control of your affairs. Many close relationships, partnerships and even marriage may be relegated to the back burner in order for you to do what you want to do, when you want to do it. This new determination of how you go about things will make you more practical than you have been. A stubborn edge will come into play quite often and people around you will start to look to you to see how you get things done. So, it isn't all bad news but do take it easy when you feel you yourself getting het up over nothing in particular. New and different ways of doing things will come into being; tradition or the old ways may not always appeal.

On 7 July 2025 Uranus moves into Gemini for about four months. You will begin to look at how you can re-organise how things could be done and one of the answers will involve communication at all levels. However, hardly any of these ideas will get under way or properly started when Uranus moves back into Taurus again for around five months or so.

Uranus retreats back into Taurus on 8 November 2025. Much of what went on before will start to surface again but won't really get under way because Uranus will move on again to the next sign. This will be a short stay because on 26 April 2026 Uranus moves on again into Gemini where it will stay until long after 2030.

Uranus in Gemini is in the eighth house of Scorpio. Partnerships of all kinds will come into play one way or another. As indicated earlier, communication at all levels will start to play a large role in the way Scorpio folk will want to work. People in business for themselves may either merge with someone else or take them over altogether. Some of you will want to change private and or joint financial arrangements by either strengthening them or completely pulling out. There will be little in the way of half measures in the way any people will work. It will be all or nothing as far as they are concerned. One or two could let things slip and become involved in very close and extremely personal emotional relationships during this period.

Neptune

From 1 January 2021 Neptune will be in Pisces, the fifth house of Scorpio. This planet eases up the tensions somewhat and lends itself to pleasure, often something to do with the unusual or unconventional. This more easy-going style of life may also have a few secrets involved, as if the subjects do not want others to know exactly what might be going on. The ability to plan ahead will develop and many are likely to take up a closer interest in the world of entertainment. Try not to rely too much on intuition; facts are always the best way, even if some new ideas might need to have a touch of luck for them to materialise.

On 30 March 2025 Neptune enters Aries. Very little starts to change although your working arena does look as though you will have a lot more put on your plate. This might affect the health. Adequate rest and relaxation together with a proper diet is essential. Don't let things get out of hand; try to delegate a little more.

Neptune turns retrograde on 4 July 2025 and re-enters Pisces on 22 October 2025 for about three months. There might be a few unexpected delays or even total hold-ups at times. You really won't get a lot started again until Neptune enters Aries again on 26 January 2026, to remain there until well after 2030.

Pluto

As the period under review opens Pluto is in Capricorn and will be there for just over a year. Changes will take place, some slowly, some quite suddenly. Single and young Scorpio people will begin to change their ways. They will become more mature, more reliable and steady. The more mature Scorpio folk will begin to exert more authority in the way they work and play. Local politics may appeal and the chance to work behind the scenes in almost anything will be gratefully taken up because this is a natural place for them to work. If financial matters are involved then these are the best people to take the job.

On 23 March 2023 Pluto enters Aquarius. In this short spell, Scorpio folk will become even more determined and demanding in the way they operate. However, by the time anything starts, if at all, the planet retrogrades back into Capricorn on 11 June 2023.

Scorpio people are likely to find it hard to relax properly. They may be unable to find the time to get away from it all and have fun. Even when they do find time, something is likely to happen, causing them to postpone their arrangements. This is likely to make them more edgy than usual and a streak of the dictator will begin to emerge. By the time any of this begins to seriously affect anyone Pluto moves on and enters Aquarius again on 21 January 2024.

For almost nine months or so, Pluto in the fourth house of Scorpio will affect the domestic style of life altogether. Quite a few will consider moving while a number of will actually do so. Acquiring further property is always a plus for anyone and Scorpio people will be just making sure everything will be right for their old age. They can either rent them out and, if needs be, they can always sell the place again for the money to help keep them in the style to which they aspire.

Once again, Pluto returns into Capricorn 1 September 2024 for a bare ten weeks or so. Little, if any real effect will be noticed. Plans may have to be put on hold or a couple of delays may occur but nothing overtly serious.

Pluto moves back into Aquarius again on 19 November 2024.

Now things will start to hum for Pluto will be here until 2043, so there will be plenty of time to influence things as only Pluto can. An aptitude for research work will invade much of the individual's life and an interest in outdoor activities is also possible. This could be form a simple animal or bird watching hobby to actively taking up outdoor work in the farming industry. This is often where a Scorpio subject really does come into his or her own.

There is a love of any enterprise that serves the best interest of people in general and this sort of occupation appeals to most Scorpio subjects. Finally, try not to get so involved in any undertaking so as to become a tad "out of it" or detached from normal life. Remember this and the rest of the period will close on a happy note.

CHAPTER FIFTEEN

Sagittarius

Jupiter

For the first few months Jupiter moves back and forth between through Aquarius and Pisces, not stopping for very long in either sign. This is not an easy time to try to decipher any influence the planet could exert anywhere. When Jupiter retrogrades, it behaves like Saturn at times so, at such times it might act in a restrictive way and, as Jupiter is the natural ruler of Sagittarius, this may appear more so.

Jupiter is in Aquarius as the period opens so most Sagittarians should be able to make the most of such a beneficial placing. You have plenty of faith in your own abilities along with the will to succeed but you are an impatient character. If you don't bully them people will go with you. You may become active in all matters regarding communication and travel should feature as well. Socially, you should do well and if anyone can do this Sagittarians certainly can for it is almost an art form with most of them – especially in their later years.

Jupiter enters Pisces on 13 May 2021. The home life and all domestic affairs will vie for your attention although this won't last long for the planet will return to Aquarius on 28 July 2021.

For the next five months or so Jupiter will revert back to what was described earlier for Jupiter in this sign. In addition to what was written, try not to be too difficult with those who look to you for support. Try to learn to go along with the wishes of others more than you do at present.

As the year comes to an end, Jupiter re-enters Pisces on 29 December 2021. Once here, it picks up speed and positively whooshes through this sign. It is quite influential as it transits this Water sign. Sagittarians will be full of ideas and plans because so many different subjects hold a fascination for them that, once they put their mind to something specific, very little gets in their way as they try to achieve their objective.

When, on 10 May 2022 Jupiter moves into Aries any anxieties will ease. Agreements reached about now will give those concerned time to breathe while they take a little while to consider things in general. In most other respects, it is a largely favourable time.

Jupiter turns retrograde on 28 October 2022 to re-enter Pisces. Sagittarian's personal popularity rises upward when in this Water sign but any misjudgement or a misunderstanding made now could be quite expensive when it comes to relationship matters. Partners in such issues must respect each other but if one over-plays his or her hand it will cost them more than just a friendship; they will be left high and dry and on their own.

A few weeks later on 20 December 2022 Jupiter re-enters Aries and takes some five months to rush through this sign to enter Taurus on 16 May 2023.

Jupiter in the Sagittarian sixth house suggests that you must be very careful about your diet. If you are feeling as though things just aren't going as they should, you may console yourself with all the wrong foods in your diet and this planet here just loves rich food, so be advised. On a few odd occasions you may be temporarily embarrassed by a lack of funds – immediate cash to hand and so on. You have money but it will be all tied up where you can't get at as you might like. Take it easy, let other folk do what you can do with one hand tied behind your back. At work, changes may be introduced by those in higher positions which are largely beneficial to most. However, where there may be a few anomalies it will be Sagittarius to the rescue.

On 25 May 2024 Jupiter moves on into Gemini. Sagittarius people are never really comfortable with any major planet in their opposite sign and they tend to be rather unwilling or helpful to those who might need their advice and guidance. As a result, other folk tend to act in much the same way and there is many a stand-off in these associations at all levels. But, while this all going on, some Sagittarians will want to spread their wings somewhat. A few may explore the world of entertainment, while others may look at some areas of the church. The sporting arena may capture the interest of some and, into the bargain many single folk of both sexes will encounter romantic interests on their way.

Jupiter begins a transit of Cancer on 19 June 2025. The planet is in exaltation here and any sensitivity will certainly grow as it traverses the sign. Socially, you are quite happy to get along with most folk but in this period you will prefer people to come to you rather than actually attend most but not all functions. For some, children in some way may become a worry. The need to explore new avenues of interest will continue. Some may become interested in the law, with a few pursuing a magistrate's position at the end of a period of study. Sagittarians can be quite restless at times and it will show.

Jupiter starts to pass through Leo on 30 June 2026. Both signs get along quite well with each other so our subjects will enter into even more new avenues of leisure that Sagittarians love so much. Sport, entertainment and similar outdoor activities may be taken on. For those who prefer their comforts indoors, higher education and teaching will be assessed. For some, business connected to the world of real estate will attract. Married Sagittarians should take care, for there will be several chances to enter into romantic liaisons which, if discovered by the partner, will almost certainly end the tie.

Jupiter moves on and into Virgo on 26 July 2027, the Sagittarian tenth house. This will favour all career and occupational interests and you may be called on to mastermind rather large interests for which you have the talent and ability to show eventual success. However, this may be in conflict with one or two of your domestic arrangements. Family first is the right avenue to pursue in such cases; most managers or employers will appreciate this and bear with you.

As Jupiter starts to pass through Libra on 24 August 2028, you should begin to reap many benefits for all your hard work. Socially, you ought to shine and there may well be a few invitations to join clubs or groups that you have eyed for some time. For those in their middle years, the accumulation of all their studies and many interests really will pay off around now. They will feel as though they have "arrived" and pursue their favourite interests with a lot more zeal and enthusiasm. Career wise opportunities are likely to be offered and while not all will be taken up, those that are will prove most worthwhile.

Single Sagittarians will find a new world of love and romance open up to them and for a few here and there, an age gap or racial difference may occur but which should not be allowed to blight the potential. Jupiter in Libra can make some people promise far more than can deliver – make a note, don't get caught in that trap.

Jupiter's next move is into Scorpio on 24 September 2029. Decisions will have to be made on the right priority at times as employment and domestic arrangements may be inter-dependent on each other. You may want to move house or a promotion may need you to do so. While the partner does appreciate both sides of the question, he or she should be allowed as much room as possible to discuss and help to resolve the many issues involved. Do not make decisions without this sort of consultation.

On 22 October 2030 Jupiter begins to transit your own sign of Sagittarius. You shouldn't put a foot wrong in the short time before the end of the year. Yet a few more open doors will present themselves for you to pass through and enjoy. The older people will explore new territories eagerly but the younger folk may be a tad more suspicious or not be ready to accept anything new. As long as you are reasonably careful with your financial arrangements, all should go well. Try not to become too aloof or unapproachable by anyone in any of your capacities. Remember those who helped you on the way to where you are now.

Saturn

Saturn is in Aquarius as 2021 opens. This is the Sagittarian's third house and in this sign and house it shows how determined you will be in defining how you will live in your old age. Financially astute (even while young), many will already have some plans for their retirement in place. Developing really firm roots is almost ways a part of most Sagittarian's of life – you rarely find a poor one. Equally, these people are not in that much of a rush to marry, so they always have half an eye on what and whom they might want. Make no mistake, they miss very little.

Saturn enters Pisces on 7 March 2023 and as time wears on you will become most aware about yourself and take steps to hone the edges and rough spots until you are satisfied. Young people will be important and, if in the teaching profession of any kind, they will become even better at what they do. Elsewhere, you may not be as actively sociable and could even lack a little personal discipline at times. This will pass, but at a price. If nothing else, you do at least learn by your mistakes. If not already married, many tend to meet and begin the courting rituals of life when Saturn is here. It does not follow that you will marry and settle, only that you may do so.

Saturn moves into Aries on 25 May 2025 and you will need to take care of how you approach and deal with other people. At first, this will not be easy because you can be a tad too demanding. Little can really get under way because within a few weeks or so, Saturn turns retrograde and edges back into Pisces on 1 September 2025 for a few months. Your slightly selfish ways will gradually ease and improve.

Saturn returns into Aries on 14 February 2026 and will be here for a couple of years. A natural for business matters of many kinds, especially financial issues, you will expand your interests in the many different directions this might lead for you. Ambition, drive and a sense of achievement will grow and irrespective of age, many Sagittarians will gain in understanding others as well as themselves. Single folk are unlikely to marry during this period but it won't stop them from experimenting (?).

On 13 April 2028 Saturn enters Taurus, the Sagittarian sixth house. As they explore new areas of interest, they will leave little to chance. Their overall approach to such issues will become quite serious and a few may begin to specialise in what attracts them the most at this time. Engaged people might want to delay marriage until they feel more secure but at the same time they can't bring themselves to disappoint any future partner and that is so thoughtful and so reliable.

On 1 June 2030 Saturn edges into Gemini where it will remain long after the end of the year. Relationships of all kinds will be important. You could end up darting hither and thither ensuring that you have at least fixed things with those who you consider to be the "right" people, for what you have in mind at any rate. Behind this and whatever else you may get up to will be based on your need to feel secure. Not only that you will seem a tad austere to some but this only a passing fad.

Uranus

As the period under review opens Uranus is in Taurus where it will be for the next five years. You will appear rather too determined for some folk probably because you come over as ultra practical in much of what you do. This makes you look clever as well and some people of lesser ability tend to not like this very much but that's their problem. There is a possibility of a change of job which might involve the whole career or just be a better step forward. Ease back on the rebel streak and make sure that what you do is not too radical. Only Sagittarians can really appreciate that style of getting things done. You may discover a hidden (or re-discover an unused) talent for the arts or music and the entertainment world.

On 7 July 2025 Uranus moves into Gemini for about four months. Little, if anything will come of this until it turns retrograde in early September prior to returning to re-enter Taurus. However, there could be a hint of indecisiveness at times. Certainly your curiosity streak will begin to get quite active.

Uranus retreats back into Taurus on 8 November 2025. This will be a short stay of some five months or so and the planet will be retrograde most of the time until it turns direct again on 3 Feb 2026. When retrograde, Uranus in this house eases back any inner tensions but once it starts to move forward again these subjects should be prepared for Uranus to re-enter Gemini where it will stay until well past 2030. There will be a chance of a new romantic interest developing for Sagittarians of both sexes, whether married or not. For some this will prove to be quite dodgy while for others it may be a help in some way.

Neptune

As the period under review opens up, Neptune will be in Pisces for about four years or so. While in their fourth house Sagittarian's domestic and personal life will have many experiences, most of which will cause a few changes of thought and, in some cases, the heart as well. Home life will not be as straightforward as they might like, and any confusion or doubts they may have could surface and the whole relationship will just end. Older people, the parents perhaps, or the younger element might create problems in this area. Do think twice before you reach any decisions.

On 30 March 2025 Neptune enters Aries but won't be there for long. These subjects will want more freedom in which they can express themselves the way they want whenever they want. Single Sagittarians will enjoy a short period of romantic interchanges but when Neptune turns retrograde on 4 July 2025 to re-enter Pisces on 22 October 2025, these mini adventures will stop for a while. Life won't be quite as exciting for at least a couple of months.

But when Neptune enters Aries again on 26 January 2026, it will stay there until well after 2030. Once again, there will be much less restriction on all the activities with which these subjects just love to become involved. In the working arena many will become highly competitive and likely to initiate things that others wouldn't dare to try. Any reputation they earn here will be deserved but there is just the odd chance of someone trying to create trouble for these people. These "secret enemies" might be acting through jealousy or they could be looking to step into their shoes if they are successful in getting rid of them.

Pluto

As the period under review opens Pluto is in Capricorn and this is good financially for all Sagittarians and just about all of them will try to discard outworn or outmoded possessions, with a view to renewing where they can. Some will buy new furniture for the home, special little knick-knacks in the kitchen and, quite possibly, a new (or nearly new) car. The garden will be assessed and he or she is liable to spend many a happy hour doing what they think should be done.

Some may be called upon to handle the possessions and monies of recently deceased (family?) people. Positions of trust will be offered and accepted and these people should begin to shine socially.

On 23 March 2023 Pluto moves into Aquarius for a few weeks only. Now it is the turn for some of their relationships to be looked at and decisions made as to who they wish to stay with and who will be of little use to them. However, in this short period these may be just ideas, little will actually be done.

On 11 June 2023 Pluto retrogrades back into Capricorn. It remains this way for quite some time before it turns direct again. Any agreements made or renewed should be looked at professionally, or there could be problems these subjects cannot handle properly. Long distance travel, especially abroad is possible.

On 21 January 2024 Pluto edges back into Aquarius again for around six month or so. While normally quite traditional in their outlook, especially in the more mature years, many Sagittarians are liable to want to make changes and introduce new methods of working in the local and domestic environment. Opposition is more than likely.

Once again Pluto returns into Capricorn 1 September 2024. It will only be for a few weeks where little should be started but many older arrangements may come into being.

Pluto moves back into Aquarius again on 19 November 2024 but this time it will stay there until 2043.

For the rest of the of the time until the end of the period under review, Sagittarians will develop an inner sense of well-being and many will go from strength to strength in the career arena. Elsewhere, politics, local or national, will attract and many of these subjects will seek or be offered positions of power and or authority away from their working area. There will be much "to-ing and fro-ing" at times and the partner may well put their foot down to demand more time in the domestic vicinity. And that is where they will have to relent or risk losing quite a lot if they do not do as they are asked (told?).

CHAPTER SIXTEEN

Capricorn

Jupiter

For a while, Jupiter won't move too far because it will spend some time moving back and forth through Aquarius and Pisces. Then it will hover between Pisces and Aries. It won't be that easy to define or assess precisely what it might or might not influence in this period. It would be helpful for people to appreciate that when Jupiter performs in this manner and turns retrograde, its influence is not dissimilar to that of a forward motion Saturn, so at times it will seem to be restrictive. All subjects will have re-assessed their thinking at such times.

Jupiter is in Aquarius for the first four months of 2021, the second house for all Capricorn people. These people are well-known for their middle-of-the road ways and because of this, they are liable to make quite a new wave of friendships and associations with all manner of people, many of whom will be in a position to help them in later years. There will be financial benefits during this spell. Few Capricornians really gamble, so what they do make will go a long way into swelling their reserves. You rarely find a poor Capricorn subject – of any age.

Jupiter moves on into Pisces on 13 May 2021 and where some will try their hand in the kitchen and experiment with cooking all sorts of dishes, others make themselves useful in various types of charity work. A few might enter or move onwards and upwards in the acting/entertainment professions. Making money will not be a central issue here but somehow or another, it will seem to come to them relatively easily. If it is deemed necessary they will buy new and or useful things for their home.

On 28 July 2021 Jupiter moves back into Aquarius. Until the middle of October it will stay retrograde. This planet will seem to hold a grip on any and all plans for expansion of all kinds. By all means plan but do so only on paper until October, then try to push your ideas into being. Financial fluctuations are a possibility in this period and you ought to try to be ready – just in case.

On 29 December 2021 Jupiter moves once more into Pisces. It is time to pick up where you left off and try to continue with what occupies you the most. Jupiter in this house and sign is not wholly favourable but it is a helpful place in general. Local affairs will attract for a variety of reasons but you may have some inner uncertainty as to what you could do. You will know what you want to do but actually getting around to doing anything concrete might be beyond your present skills.

Jupiter enters Aries on May 10 2022 for just over four months. There will be a taste for home affairs of all kinds and, in a few cases there may even be a change of address or, perhaps, a few who might invest in more property for letting or there may be another idea up their sleeve. The home may be used for business purposes – working from or at home is quite the vogue of late, certainly in the UK.

On 28 October 2022 Jupiter retrogrades back into Pisces for a few weeks. Close relatives or siblings may become a nuisance. They want what Capricorn has but are probably not prepared to put themselves out in the same way. This may be the end of some relationships within the family because it is almost a racing certainty that many Capricorn folk won't lift a finger to help. Other members within the family circle would very unwise to interfere here.

It re-enters Aries on 20 December 2022 where it will be for six months. One or two might get a bee in their bonnet about something that does not quite meet with their approval, or the complete reverse, and worry about the business until it does. Jupiter here can often create this situation. At such times, Capricornians are advised to exercise caution because unforeseen circumstances can occur.

On 16 May 2023 Jupiter enters Taurus and will be here for a year. This can indicate much closer personal relationships between all types of couples whether single or married. The ladies may or may not wish to become pregnant which is one of the possibilities. Money, position and possessions will be high on the agenda for a lot of Capricorn people. While they are normally quite astute with their finances this is one occasion when they are prepared to spend, but only on the good things (in their eyes) of life. It would best to advise them that it isn't actual money, possessions or status that is important but what they actually do with such things.

On 25 May 2024 Jupiter edges into Gemini to stay for a year. Practically anything new will attract and the world of communication especially so. The career, the people with whom they work or associate with, both in their own company or that of others, will help to widen Capricorn's interests. This will help them develop a much better overall attitude all round. If any changes are to be implemented, they may be directed toward the younger element. Capricorn people make excellent teachers, as long as they are properly trained. It is not beyond the possibility that some of you might take up the profession as a complete change from your present career.

Jupiter begins a transit of Cancer on 9 June 2025 and the planet is in exaltation here. In this sign Jupiter manages whatever subjects are concerned (in this case Capricorn) to become more mature in their overall outlook and manner. Almost anything to do with the Capricorn home and domestic life will become accentuated as the time wears on. Youngsters are likely to play a more prominent role while these young folk tend to become much closer to their own parents or other older members of the family. People involved in the services industries will flourish and a few not already in this area may elect to do so. Generally speaking, this should be an all-round profitable period in many ways. As Jupiter in Cancer relates strongly to food and the kitchen in general, a few of them may begin to experiment in this area. A word of warning however, should this come about with you and yours, try to remember the waistline.

The great planet begins its journey through Leo on 30 June 2026. If nothing else, Capricorn people will shine with an increased sense of leadership and self-confidence throughout this spell. They will develop a greater fondness for young people, their own or those of others. Some may even take up a spare time activity to ensure young people learn how to handle the necessary problems maturity and adulthood bring. These people will become known for their energy and the way they know how to handle entertaining at home. There will be much financial activity one way or another. In many cases all should go well but there may be an odd occasions where such matters become a tad difficult. These may range from simple joint monetary arrangements to serious tax issues that will take some sorting out.

On 26 July 2027 Jupiter enters Virgo. Travel for business or pleasure will be a feature of this new period with the possibility of dealing with places or people from abroad. There may be a few problems trying to match detail with an expansive inner nature with the need to delegate. You will have to remember to compromise with the extremes of requirements that may be your lot in the working arena. One helpful point will be the way you and colleagues of all levels tend to get on.

On 24 August 2028 Jupiter moves into Libra. The basic principles of where credit is due will apply. As a rule, you are pretty fair when it comes to this sort of thing but there will be an occasion or two when you will have to convince others. The more balanced your relationships are, the happier you will be. Within your domestic circle, you may be called upon to take charge of the celebration for a possible birth, anniversary or even a wedding. If it does occur, it may well be before the turn of the year. In early 2029 some extensive short journeys may have to be made, probably more for personal reasons than for business purposes.

Jupiter enters Scorpio on 24 September 2029. This will bring a period of intense emotional occasions. Money matters matter and there will be a need to "examine the books" in all of your activities. This isn't exactly a time for a turn out but you may feel inclined to think and act that way. There will be a number of changes that you may want to make within your social circles. Some may be new; others will be updated, while what is left may be thought to be of little use. These changes often take place when Jupiter passes through Scorpio almost as a matter of course. This can make a few enemies but you will know how to deal with them. Nevertheless, it looks as though it is going to be one of "those" years.

Jupiter moves on into Sagittarius on 22 October 2030. Between now and the end of 2030, little will get a chance to get under way. However, there is remote possibility that your working conditions may change because of domestic issues. There is an equally remote opportunity to look at the state of the financial markets and start, probably privately at first, to look ahead and predict the potential here.

Saturn

Saturn is in Aquarius as 2021 opens where it will remain for just over two years. There will be an increased level of concentration and the Capricornians will become a lot more organised in the way they operate at work. Financially, they should increase their income for they will work even harder than before. They like (and want) the better things of life. If they are in any way unable to achieve their aim during this period, a member of their family may well offer to help out. At work, there could be an improvement in how and where they work. The company may be looking for new premises. A few may have to re-assess their domestic relationships and climb down a bit.

Saturn enters Pisces on 7 March 2023. In this third house Saturn is likely to affect the way these people work. If they don't like what is happening, some may change direction or their job altogether. Whatever happens, the art of communication at one level or another will come into play. Capricorn folk aren't that keen on travelling too much for any reason, which is another possible cause for such changes to come into effect. If at any time the subject has to make agreements of any kind, he or she must exercise caution before they agree to anything. Run whatever it is before the right people and, once they have said it is OK to do so, go ahead.

Saturn moves into Aries on 25 May 2025. You are going to have to put all family and domestic issues first and foremost through-out this spell. Work must take second place or you risk heavy losses in the personal life. Spend less time out and about and concentrate more on you and yours. Concentrate a little less on past issues and worry more about the here and now. It wouldn't hurt to become a tad more circumspect about your health and associated diet.

On 1 September 2025 Saturn retrogrades back into Pisces. When it is retrograde motion, this planet can sometimes appear to ease back on any of its restrictions and allow you to move forward at a reasonable pace. In the event go with this. It will only be for about four months and it would be unwise for any misunderstanding to occur during this period.

Saturn moves back into Aries on 14 February 2026. For just over two years, Saturn is now free to influence what it will and how it will and the advice given earlier still holds.

On 13 April 2028 Saturn enters Taurus. The ladies should be careful to keep an eye on their health at all times for this does not favour them too well. It may be nothing too serious, if anything does come about or it might be quite an issue at other times. Both sexes need to keep a weather eye on the way they relate to their partners and people in their social circles. The younger element are advised to make sure that if they do have problems, they should make certain they can't handle them before they approach their elders within the family circle.

On 1 June 2030 Saturn edges into Gemini but is hardly there for any real time for Saturn to wield any real influence. However, a strongly practical streak will start to develop but it must not be allowed to get out of hand.

Uranus

As the period under review opens, Uranus is in Taurus. For some time to come, your monetary arrangements, banking and general status is going to change somewhat for the better. You will see the beginning of a period of changes. Some are likely to be a tad drastic in the way that they suddenly occur. You will manage these changes with your usual shrewd way with such things. Inwardly, you might not like it but outwardly few will know this. Just be ready for the tax man and whether he (or she) is right or wrong. Investments scheduled to finalise in the coming years may prove better than originally visualised. As time progresses, you may become more and more interested in the world of entertainment. This may well be in the behind-the-scenes business and financial matters. As you become more independent, it looks as though you might venture into this area.

On 7 July 2025 Uranus moves into Gemini for a short period. This favours those who like to work more in the background but along with others of a similar ilk at the same time. There will be very little time for anything to get under way but you can still lay a few plans.

Uranus retreats back into Taurus on 8 November 2025. It will stay here for a short while of some six months or so. The planet will be retrograde most of the time until it turns direct again on 3 Feb 2026. When retrograde, Uranus in this house inclines people to slightly unconventional behaviour patterns and can make a few quite unpredictable even by those who know them well.

On 26 April 2026 Uranus moves on again into Gemini. Now not only can you lay your plans as you see fit, you have another four years or so to make something of them. There is a possibility of a job change or a new direction in your career altogether, although much will depend on what and how much work or responsibility you may be asked to undertake.

Neptune

As the period opens, Neptune is in Pisces and for the next ten years, the planet will move back and forth between here and Aries. While direct in Pisces Capricorn people are likely to become interested in the church, mysticism and other fringe matters. Some may become involved in astrology or similar arts. Whatever business issues that directly affect you and your career come into being, you will handle them all with great caution, almost as if you might not fully trust what was going on.

On 30 March 2025 Neptune enters Aries for about three months. Certain domestic arrangements could go adrift, although there is hardly time for Neptune to really influence anything. Once it turns retrograde on 4 July 2025, it could affect the fuel system but this may not happen in the time available, for it re-enters Pisces on 22 October 2025. Most things should be relatively quiet until a few weeks later, when it moves into Aries again on 26 January 2026 and will stay there until well after 2030 has passed.

Pluto

As the period starts, Pluto is in Capricorn. There won't be too much worry or concern with your own welfare and those of your close family ties but there will be an anxious eye on the state of what might or could be happening in the world in general. Pluto here is unsettling for both the individual and the outside world. So, you will develop a higher level of awareness as changes occur. The political world may come over as unable to function as it should. A rather highly charged sense of power is likely to come about. Should one or two matters take place, they are likely to be dealt with by you in a rather unconventional way.

On 23 March 2023 Pluto enters Aquarius for a few weeks. Little will really happen and the planet will retrograde back into Capricorn on 11 June 2023. Your social life will experience a few changes perhaps and there will be a hint of a rebel streak beginning to form. Some six months later on 21 January 2024,

Pluto edges back into Aquarius again. In this short stay, Pluto will exercise a few muscles here and there but nothing overtly solid should take place.

Once again, Pluto returns into Capricorn on 1 September 2024 for a relatively brief period and then a few weeks later it moves into Aquarius again on 19 November 2024 to stay until 2043.

This next six years are going to be quite enlightening for Capricorn people. Socially, there will be a lot of changes going on with an equal amount of uncertainty as to exactly what is happening. Closer to home, there will be a number of changes implemented by you in your financial arrangements. Joint agreements may be terminated for any number of reasons, the most important of which will be that you want sole responsibility all the time.

CHAPTER SEVENTEEN

Aquarius

Jupiter

Initially, Jupiter hovers between Aquarius and Pisces and will not be too easy to assess what it might or might not influence at these times. Hopefully, the majority of Aquarians will appreciate this. When Jupiter acts this way and turns retrograde, its influence is not too different from that of a forward moving Saturn, so at times it might appear to be a tad restrictive. Aquarians will need to understand this and re-assess their thinking at such times.

Jupiter is in Aquarius for the first four months of 2021 and, when in the first house, Jupiter influences the subject to be rather self-willed and reasonably tolerant. Aquarians are likely to go off at a tangent at times but as a rule, they can be a shade too impartial when called upon to make a decision. If you are one of those who were an early success story, people will look to you for leadership, should the need arise.

Aquarians should watch their diet and health for they may start to put on weight. Once on, they will have to work very hard to shed even a pound. One or two may find they have to travel more than usual because of the business calls on their time.

Jupiter enters Pisces on 13 May 2021 but will not remain here for long. However, even in this short spell, money matters will seem to become easier to understand. Making money won't be central so much but cash may come in a tad faster than before.

Aquarians will have to handle these increases with more attention to the detail necessary.

On 28 July 2021 Jupiter re-enters Aquarius and until the mid-October it will remain retrograde. When it travels in this fashion, the planet will appear to allow fluctuations of income and expenditure without much warning.

On 29 December 2021 Jupiter returns to Pisces. While some might think it is time to pick up where they left off, others won't seem to have the will or whatever to continue as they did. However, some may well now start to go from strength to strength and secure quite a few useful assets. Others may just fade out of the hard drive and just let life pass them by.

Jupiter moves into Aries on 10 May 2022 to stay for a shade over four months. In this sign, the planet is likely to influence these subjects in a most positive manner. The will be a strong increased sense of optimism and, although inclined to be a little impulsive, others will still seek their advice and guidance.

On 28 October 2022, Jupiter turns retrograde and passes back to Pisces for just a few weeks. A touch of prudence will be needed, if not by the Aquarians then by their partners. Extra travel may call, so the need to plan well ahead will be necessary.

Jupiter gets going on the move again and enters Aries on 20 December 2022, this time to stay for about six months. Pride and prejudice is going to almost sweep in this time. The efforts of Aquarians of either sex might be called into question, mostly because of their attitude. They may seem more interested in their own advancement than what is in front of them, especially where it might aid the competition. A change of job is possible or, for a limited time only, one or two might try or be called to handle two positions at the same time.

On 16 May 2023, Jupiter starts a transit of Taurus to stay for a year. Family life and the whole domestic scene will need very careful handling for all Aquarians, possibly because of some neglect while they pursue other matters. Arguments and discussions will arise between partners because the Aquarian might want to work at or from the home. This could involve a certain amount of entertaining in the home. Provided whatever needs doing is completed properly first, this may be (grudgingly) agreed.

On 25 May 2024 Jupiter starts to pass through Gemini, which will take it just over a year to complete. If the Aquarian does start to work in the domestic area, he or she will need to brush up on their computer and communication knowledge. Emails will flow back and forth quite strongly, so they are going to either learn or be taught the tricks of this particular trade. The creative arts, the interests and needs of the younger element or offspring will become important and there could be a series of joint monetary matters talked about and actually got under way. The social life will become busier, along with a growing interest in local affairs and, for some, local politics. Aquarians are going to become quite active.

Jupiter begins to pass through Cancer on 9 June 2025 and in exaltation in this sign, which will prove to be a great help to many Aquarians. While it largely favours the older Aquarian, many of the younger element will begin to more fully understand the various aspects of the business world. It won't be long before they start to implement some of this knowledge, which should put them on the right promotion track. One or two might gravitate to the catering area or become interested in the welfare world.

The great planet starts to transit through Leo on 30 June 2026. Single people might find the right partner during this period and marriage is on the cards for many Aquarians of all ages. A better sense of fair play and the right way to do things will also develop. Outdoor pursuits may become of more of an interest. Sport, perhaps where animals may be concerned or actual country working, perhaps where animals may be involved in some way. For something completely different, a few may become useful somewhere in the background within the world of the performing arts.

On 26 July 2027 Jupiter enters Virgo. This can create a few problems for those close to these subjects. Some may overdo the adherence to detail and the proper attitude. Others can just as easily go the other way and develop a lazy streak second to none.

However, both types are likely to treat health problems a little more seriously than usual – they may start a diet to gain or lose weight according to the way they view themselves. The holiday season could involve travel for fun by literally just going where they fancy at the time and stopping over in B&B places as and when.

On 24 August 2028 Jupiter enters Libra to stay for just over a year. Aquarians will shine in the coming period because of the way they can mediate or negotiate and mediate. These gifts will be known to the employers and they will know how and when to bring these subjects in to settle any outstanding business problems. This would also be a good time to use Aquarians for opening talks with people or companies based abroad. A few might be transferred to a training program because of the way they can teach people.

When Jupiter enters Scorpio on 24 September 2029 there is likely to be some competition for a few promotional possibilities open to them. They are advised not to overplay their hands too much. Some will develop difficult personality traits; conceit, over-confidence and an almost "it's mine" attitude to any postings. Elsewhere, Aquarians must be careful of how they deal with the opposite sex, for there is a danger of (secret?) liaisons forming that can only create more problems later. Straight-laced bosses may react by firing those involved. Therefore, for those who care, career matters matter.

Jupiter enters Sagittarius on 22 October 2030 but won't have a lot of time to influence much. However, in this short time left, these subjects may become aware that their social life begins to widen. Their popularity among the local environment will grow and there will be more calls on their time.

Saturn

Saturn is in Aquarius at the start of 2021 and will be there for just over two years. Aquarians will have started to have been aware of a certain amount of restriction, for it hasn't really started to affect anything. It only went into Aquarius in December 2020. Some may have thought about how tradition or the accepted ways of getting things started could be almost a barrier to what could be achieved once a project was under way. However, as time wears on, these subjects will start to feel more self-confident and self-assured as they get things moving – their way.

Saturn in this sign makes the individuals of either sex more practical. When this is combined with a gifted imagination and the ability to tackle new problems in a satisfactory manner, they will become much more amenable and approachable to all concerned. In late May 2021 Saturn turns retrograde for a short while until the October. This could prove to be quite convenient. These people can now look at what they started to see if they can make any more changes. If there is a way, they will find it and do the necessary.

Saturn moves into Pisces on 7 March 2023. In this second house of Aquarius, Saturn will help the individual ease up a little and attend more to his or her financial arrangements. Their business acumen will mature because of their growing resourcefulness. They value what they have and they don't like to lose a penny, even if means a pound coming in later on.

Saturn enters Aries on 25 May 2025 for around three month or so. This "taster" might have a few Aquarians think about properly attending or studying certain facets of their work to gain a better understanding that the practical side has allowed. If they word this correctly to the right people, they may well be allowed to pursue their idea.

On 1 September 2025 Saturn retrogrades back into Pisces. When it is retrograde, Saturn will seem to have relaxed its grip on one or two things. These people can discuss more freely with their partners the "ins and outs" of joint financial arrangements and actually get something under way.

Saturn advances back into Aries on 14 February 2026. For around two years or so, Saturn will now be free to influence what it will and how it will. This planet in direct motion will create a slightly more severe or mature outlook. This could be at the cost of a lack of consideration of and for other people who work or socialise with them.

On 13 April 2028 Saturn moves into Taurus. Once in the fourth Aquarian house Saturn these people will become a tad too controlled and even controlling in some cases. They won't allow anyone to interfere and any advice offered may not be heeded. There could be a quite definite line drawn between career and domestic issues that the partners will not like at all. As a result, there will be a few differences that will need to be properly discussed and acted upon. The Aquarian must adopt a more balance outlook on life otherwise he or she are set to lose more than they can really afford in more ways than one.

Saturn begins to transit Gemini on 1 June 2030. However, in the six months to the end of the period little is likely to get under way, other than a need to look out for the needs of the younger element in the family. If they are too austere or logical, they might undermine whatever good they may try to carry out.

Uranus

As the year begins, Uranus is in transit in Taurus for the next four and a half years or so. Overall, there will be a hint of a stubborn nature that will come through occasionally, as a few Aquarians resent some implications in respect of some of their financial dealings. Mostly though, the principal feature over the next four and a half years will be in and around the domestic scene. Changes are going to come about. Youngsters will fly the nest to set up home for themselves or with others. There may well be a host of home improvements in the offing. A decision as to whether to extend where they are or move altogether will also need to be made. Some Aquarians may want to change career direction as well and what they might choose would almost certainly require a complete change of scenery. Long-suffering partners may well make their own decision and not go with them.

On 7 July 2025 Uranus moves into Gemini for a short period. This favours those who like to work on new projects, just to get them up and running. And that may be as far as they go, because they tend to get bored easily. However, the planet hardly has time to manoeuvre anything.

Uranus re-enters Taurus on 8 November 2025 to stay for about six months. It will also be retrograde for a short while until it moves direct again on 3 Feb 2026. When retrograde, Uranus here implies people to become a tad unpredictable unconventional behaviour patterns so much so that, at times, even those who know them well won't be too sure of what is going on. The old business of domestic of planned or unplanned upheavals will not be far away either.

On 26 April 2026 Uranus moves on again into Gemini where it will stay for the rest of the period under review. Some of the plans can now become a reality and once Uranus really does get under way, these subjects are likely to become interested in the engineering world. Some Aquarians may awaken talents hitherto unrealised as they discover they have a flair for all sorts of business and social matters in their old interests.

Neptune

Neptune is in Pisces in January 2021 and over the next ten years it will move back and forth between here and Aries. While direct in Pisces Aquarians it will involve these subjects to become more interested in the financial scene and some possessions that money can buy. For some, money will simply come and go while for others joint enterprises will seem to be the best way forward. Clever investments now will reap the right rewards later.

On 30 March 2025 Neptune enters Aries for about three months. Some questionable as against impractical thinking is likely but a slow-moving planet like this can hardly influence anything such a short time.

It turns retrograde on 4 July 2025 and while this way Aquarians might easily become a shade over sensitive but few if any may be so affected for the planet is hardly here before it moves once again into Pisces on 22 October 2025. Some interest may be shown in the world of creative arts. Some muddled thinking may also occur but in the three months or so that the planet is in this sign little of anything serious is likely to happen.

On 26 January 2026 and will stay there until well after 2030 has passed. There may be a few clever ideas that others could soon hone into a practical reality. One or two may like the idea of more travel for business or pleasure. Aquarians should be careful how they get along with others, for there will be a chance of selfishness creeping into their thinking and actions that others close to them won't want to tolerate for long. If there are any siblings who may require their help,, it will depend rather largely on whether they are all still in touch with each other. If they just drift in and out of their life, this might depend on the mood of the Aquarian concerned.

Pluto

On 1 January 2021 Pluto is two thirds of the way through Capricorn and will turn retrograde in late April. About five months later, it turns direct again in late October. This will be a year where a brick wall may in some cases just be made of sand while at other times it really will be a solid affair. Much of what Aquarians may want to do could so easily be thwarted because of Pluto's erratic motion. In Capricorn, the planet tends to influence the emotional life in such a way that the subjects involved might just bend the rules to get their own way. And if anyone can do it and get away with it, Aquarians certainly can.

On 23 March 2023 Pluto enters Aquarius for just a few weeks but very little will come of this because on 11 June 2023 it returns to Capricorn. New hobbies and past times may take up some their spare time but this is such a short spell all it may do is possibly influence a romantic interlude outside the present life style.

Almost six months later on 21 January 2024 Pluto edges back into Aquarius again for another short stay. In the eight months or so it is here, both male and female subjects will endeavour to spread their social wings a little more than usual. They normally set great store by friendships at all levels and for all purposes. In their own sign Pluto may also strive to change personal appearances.

Yet again Pluto returns into Capricorn. This will be on 1 September 2024 for a relatively brief period for just a few weeks later it moves into forward into Aquarius on 19 November 2024 and will stay there until 2043.

This will be quite a fascinating few years for Aquarians in general. In their first house, this planet will engender more interest in their own personal power and influence at work and in their social lives. All forms of technology will begin to take up some of their time either in theory or, for some, in actual practice, if sufficiently captivated. Ambitions will become a lot stronger and, in quite a few cases they could be ruthless as they progress.

In early May 2025 it will turn retrograde for around six months. At this time, they really would be best advised to put as much as they can on hold, otherwise they may go overboard and be unable to get back to where they were. Pluto moves retrograde again several times before the end of the period and the same advice is offered.

CHAPTER EIGHTEEN

Pisces

Jupiter

As 2021 opens, Jupiter is in Aquarius for around four months or so. Pisces people are rather sensitive souls at the best of times and this planet in their twelfth house suggests a need to shrug off old or expected ideas and behaviour pattern others feel should be kept. Many may prefer not to get too involved with others unless it would be considered rude to do so. Some of you should think twice before becoming involved in a close liaison outside marriage. Money matters will need your firm hand on the tiller and there could be any number of different ideas on how to invest some of your assets for best results later. However much you may dislike to feel responsible for your present position in life, you must not think of giving any of it up. Just take things easy for a while.

Jupiter enters Pisces on 13 May 2021. Once in your own sign, this planet will influence much of what you do. Remember to watch your diet or health and weight problems could arise. Jupiter won't be here that long, so just make sure you follow the rules.

On 28 July 2021 Jupiter moves back into Aquarius for just on five months. All that was discussed for this position may be read above.

On 29 December 2021 Jupiter moves once more into Pisces. An ever increasing sense of optimism is likely to develop. There will be a growing desire to want to travel, not long distances so much as just getting away from too regular a routine you might consider a tad boring at times. A few Pisceans will either continue to pursue their aims as before or try to do so away from the limelight. You will probably prefer to keep out of your expected social obligations, unless you really have to do so.

Jupiter moves into Aries on May 10 2022 for just over four months. This is a splendid house for Pisces people. Some will adopt a "front" in business issues, especially if they have their own companies. Their financial status will become much easier to manage and they will develop a steady and progressive career path. A competitive and slightly impulsive attitude will develop. In late July the planet will turn retrograde prior to moving back into Pisces. When retrograde in the second house, Jupiter may influence a tendency to slacken off and delay necessary actions in the money arena.

On 28 October 2022 Jupiter retrogrades back into Pisces for a few weeks, where it hardly has the time to influence anything of any serious or long term effect in any direction. It moves direct again in late November and enters Aries again on 20 December 2022, where it will be for six months. It will pass through this sign quite quickly and as it does so it will trigger off on or two rather helpful issues for you. Becoming more adaptable will be one clear effect and an ability to dream up new concepts or re-worked old thinking brought up to date in the career or business arenas.

On 16 May 2023 Jupiter enters Taurus and will be here for a year. Your normally alert and rather active attitude to life will develop more humour. There may be a desire to want to move house or enlarge what you already have. This may be triggered off if other members of the family express a desire or the need to want to move in for whatever reasons they may have. You and your partner will have to review this very carefully indeed before you commit one way or the other. If others do move in, they may be extremely difficult to move on if anything should go awry with the plans you make.

On 25 May 2024 Jupiter edges into Gemini to stay for a year. Changes to the home or a completely new address will once again be considered, although this time something more concrete may come forth out of any family discussion. This could also be when one of the family might turn to either working at home or from it. There would have to be some changes if this becomes the case. The often sedate type of person is likely to show a more broadminded approach to life and be quite versatile especially in and around the home. A few might be more inclined to acquaint themselves with the ins and outs of the home computer. Once they start this sort of thing, there will be no end as to what they may get up to next.

Jupiter begins a transit of Cancer on 9 June 2025. This is the sign of exaltation for this planet, for it is so much at home here. The older Pisces people know how to be good hosts, how to mix their guests when they have social affairs in the home or just have a small gathering of friends around. Jupiter in the fifth house of Pisces tends to influence their ability to handle money from simple cash issues right through to investment matters. Younger Pisces females are inclined to think of adding to their family circle or, if they already have any offspring, they become more interested in their welfare. Any spare time activity or small local work may involve young people.

The great planet begins its journey through Leo on 30 June 2026. Pisces people rarely seek the limelight but when Jupiter is in this sign, many turn to the creative or performing arts. Pisces people make good actors and actresses and this part of life could well attract a few to this sort of work. The sporting arena can also attract these subjects and they might prove to be quite good with animals in this area if given the chance. The diet conscious ladies often start weight-watching around this period as well. Both sexes have a way of just quitting a position or an arrangement if or when they feel unfairness, bullying or injustice is in the air.

On 26 July 2027 Jupiter enters Virgo. Traditionally Virgo is a sign of service and the opposite house to Pisces in a chart When Jupiter is here these people start to look at work or other positions where they feel they can be the best use for the benefit of others. The legal profession workers of all kinds are likely to get a step up.

People in the public eye lean more to charity work, while those who teach in some way start to very well indeed. As a rule, these subjects tend to appear far more severe than they actually are but they are always most discreet and can always be trusted.

On 24 August 2028 Jupiter moves into Libra. Unless you are a reasonable and fair minded individual you will never do business with Pisces folk. They are extremely selective as to whom they will act or work as a partner. This is a good time for employers to use their Pisces people to open talks with new contacts with people from abroad. They make excellent negotiators and rather formidable mediators when their services are called upon. If they have to, they can sell sand to the Arabs.

Jupiter enters Scorpio on 24 September 2029. Here is a possible fall from grace for some especially those who engage in liaisons with people outside of their current relationship, like an "eternal triangle" affair for example. Jupiter transiting this water sign is where Pisces people can so easily go off the rails. This is a very strong materialistic area and, while Pisces folk do well in most practical matters, here is where they are at their weakest and, curiously, they can also become quite narrow minded during this period.

Jupiter moves on into Sagittarius on 22 October 2030 but is hardly here long enough to create any real influence before the end of the year. Their weakest point will be an inclination to gamble, sometimes just a small flutter but occasionally it could be something quite big.

Saturn

Saturn is in Aquarius as 2021 opens and will be here for just over two years. The element of restriction will be strong as you try to establish your responsibilities with your ordinary social obligations. There may be an occasion or two when you will have to use devious means to gain a point. Much will be determined by the amount of self-will you can manage to raise. There will be occasions when Pisces people will prove a tad difficult to understand or approach. It will be at times like this when a few their tried and trusted friends will simply give up and fade out of your life altogether.

Saturn enters Pisces on 7 March 2023. Saturn in your own sign is likely to incline you to a rather serious set of rules while you wend the path you want. Serious-minded and even austere at times, some Pisces people will need someone on whom they can rely for plain and straightforward advice when they need it the most. Many Pisces folk will achieve quite a few of their aims but they may also try to ride rough-shod over the wrong people. Cooperation will be almost the last thing they can get from anyone unless they relax more. They must learn that others also live in this world because, if they don't, it's going to be a rough two years. Watch your health and try to maintain a proper diet or you may lose or gain weight if not careful.

Saturn moves into Aries on 25 May 2025 and will turn retrograde in July until it re-enters Pisces later in the year. Little will be seriously influenced at this visit, for Saturn won't get far in the time available. Family members may not seem as friendly or helpful as they might normally be.

On 1 September 2025 Saturn retrogrades back into Pisces and will be here for just over four months. We have dealt with what might or might not occur earlier. In addition, take care if travelling in unfamiliar places. If someone gives instruments of any kind for Christmas, make sure you know how to use them, for you could be slightly accident prone.

Saturn moves forward to enter into again Aries on 14 February 2026 and will be here for just over two years. This period will help revive any flagging monetary matters. Business negotiations should be a doddle for you because you simply won't give much away at all when it comes to the details. Others will look to you for leadership here and you could even be offered a new position because of your obvious abilities in this field. Do try to recognise scam artists and their "get-rich-quick" schemes. Try to balance your attitude to those who have to associate with you.

On 13 April 2028 Saturn enters Taurus and this will lead to an interesting couple of years. Once in your third house, Saturn will influence the methods you employ to achieve your aims. It will help to keep you well-controlled most of the time. Where you have to negotiate anything new, take the time to read and, if needs be, re-read the paperwork before you sign anything. This is going to be a rather favourable period – make the most of it.

On 1 June 2030 Saturn edges into Gemini, where it will remain for some time. In the six months to the end of the period under review, it will influence much of what you do and want to do in your domestic arena. Your partner will need to be kept on his or her feet just to keep up because you will be a tad set in your ways. There is a remote chance of moving house. The idea here will be more for investment purposes than anything else, so it will be a question of weighing up the "pro's and con's" of such an upheaval. Some old projects, probably financial, may end in this period. You will need to ask yourself if you really want to start anything new.

Uranus

As the period under review opens, Uranus will be in the fourth house of Pisces, which is Taurus. For the next five and a half years, the main influence here will probably see many changes in the way these subjects view the many different facets of life in general. Business matters might well create a lot of travel for you. The decision to handle such things at a distance might not be a good idea in your eyes, so you will travel to the other company and make your presence felt that way. The only adverse probability is that you will have some trouble concentrating on single issues because your mind will be so active. Delegation isn't one of your strong points but it will give you a chance to test some of the people around you. For you, this will be a new method of organising people in a different manner and it does seem to be a successful idea.

On 7 July 2025 Uranus moves into Gemini for about four months. A gradual flair for the world of communication in all its different forms will attract and there may be a threat of quite a few changes to come about in the domestic area. Nothing really serious will get under way, for this planet won't be here long enough to influence much.

Uranus retreats back into Taurus on 8 November 2025. This will be a short stay of some six months or so and the planet will be retrograde most of the time until it turns direct again on 3 Feb 2026. When retrograde, Uranus in this house suggests that people will tend to shy away from conventional social obligations for no real reason, other than to want to spend more time at home or doing what they want to, when they want to it.

On 26 April 2026 Uranus moves on again into Gemini. For the next four years there will be quite a change in the character and personality of Pisces people. They will want more freedom for themselves and are likely to change their interests and hobbies until they finally find something that will occupy their mind. For some, this could be a whole new change of endeavour altogether. It might even mean a move away from their familiar area and territory where they might take up all kinds of new career ideas. Farming or associate country business matters might attract. The service industries might be another. At the end of the exercise, they will be quite happy but they might also have a fair amount of broken relationships strewn about all over the place if they do go on this tack.

Neptune

As the period under review opens up, Neptune is in Pisces. This is extremely helpful because this is your ruling planet and in your first house where it rules the personality, your image and your feelings and your overall disposition. Later, when it moves forward into Aries, it will be in your house of money, income and expenditure and your (movable) material possessions.

For the next four years or so, your deepest feelings, the way you think and your psychological appreciation of the world in general will be heightened. You need to be on your guard and not allow yourself to be caught up in any scandal. The opportunity to become more than just friendly with people will almost always be present so think before you act. The pursuit of pleasure is one thing but there may be a heavy price to pay if it such an escapade should ever become public knowledge. In practically all other (more material) matters you should become quite successful if you apply yourself diligently to what is expected of you.

On 30 March 2025 Neptune enters Aries but it will only be here for about five months. When in the second house Neptune inclines the subject to be more open with other people. He or she will be quite an individualist at times and there will be more than just subtle changes in their income and expenditure until early July when Neptune turns retrograde.

You may feel a tad "out-of-it" at times but by the time this happens (if at all) the planet will turn retrograde on 4 July 2025 and eventually re-enter Pisces on 22 October 2025. It will be back here for barely three months when it will move forward again into Aries.

Neptune enters Aries again on 26 January 2026 and will stay there until well after 2030 has passed. The ability to acquire almost what you want as your income settles into a more regular way may affect some with a slightly selfish streak. Direct financial speculation should be avoided – even an occasional little flutter. The best way forward for all Pisces people will be to invest what they can afford now for later times.

Pluto

As the period under review opens, Pluto is in Capricorn where the main influence could be where relatives play a larger role than usual. Monetary matters or their state in general may be offered for you to look after on their behalf. Career matters will be of the greatest importance over the next two years or so. Someone may help you to realise a long held ambition. There will a few times when you become unapproachable as you get so caught up with what you are doing.

On 23 March 2023 Pluto enters Aquarius, your twelfth house where ordinarily you might tend to become a shade more reclusive at times. However, Pluto will hardly be here for long enough to influence anything for it retrogrades back into Capricorn on 11 June 2023 for about six months. Little will have time to get under way but you may become inclined to change some of your friends and acquaintances for reasons best known to yourself.

On 21 January 2024 Pluto edges back into Aquarius again to stay for about seven months. Once again, there is little room for any manoeuvre or real influence to get under way. Pluto returns into Capricorn on 1 September 2024 for a few weeks and then, finally, moves back into Aquarius again on 19 November 2024 to stay until 2043. For the next few years, just about anything that catches your eye will attract your interest. A preoccupation with the unusual (astrology, palmistry, etc.) might also happen. This could also be a time to discard some of the old in favour of the new in almost every area of your life.

CHAPTER NINETEEN

Special Events

In this final chapter we can look ahead, for those (mostly rare) occasions when some of the planets appear to line up in an unusual way, make interesting or rather rare aspects to each other and view other times when people should encourage or avoid certain actions. We will deal with what astrologers call a stellium first.

The Stellium

A stellium is when a group of at least four or more planets appear to line up in a series of multiple conjunctions or are "enclosed" within a 20° arc usually in one house and or a sign. Occasionally, these planets may be in different houses and or signs but are still connected in the same way. Alternatively, where these planets may not be connected in an accepted aspect or aspects note whether the planets concerned do at least all line up to within a 20° arc. More than one stellium is usually referred to as stellia. The word comes down to us from the rather ancient and no longer used term "satellitium".

When any of the above situations occurs it suggests a heightened focus in respect of the house(s) or sign(s) in which the stellium forms. It is also thought that this phenomenon enhances the features associated with the topics of the house or the qualities of the sign to be more prominent in the subject's life. Such influences could be said to dominant factors in the chart as a whole.

In recent times probably the most famous and widely anticipated at the time was the eight-planet stellium that occurred in February 1962, when some astrologers forecasted the end of the world. A few suggested it could mean the new Messiah would be born, while others thought that it was a very special date in that it heralded the start of the Age of Aquarius. Prior to this,there was a seven-planet stellium on March 24 1762, another one on April 1 1821 in Pisces, and another on Jan 13 1831 in Capricorn. After this, there was an eight-planet stellium on May 3 1882 in Capricorn.

Between then and the present time, astrological stellia have come and gone more or less unnoticed but there has been nothing to match those just mentioned. There have been plenty of four- or five-planet stellia but nothing of great importance because the Moon has been involved in most of them.

However, there will be four six-planet stellia in the ten years under review starting with the first one on Jan 12 2021 spread through late Capricorn/early Aquarius. The next will be on Feb 3 the same year but with different planets this time all in Aquarius. On Mar 28 2025 there will be a six-planet stellium mostly in Aries. This will be followed later in 2026 with another six-planet stellium mostly in Capricorn.

There will be a seven-planet line up in Gemini in June 2032 which will be studied at some length by astrologers all over the world because it looks like a quite a fascinating array of planets mostly in Gemini.

The stellium or a series of multiple conjunctions are acknowledged by astrologers to denote a fusion of the power and influence of each planet concerned. You have read in earlier chapters of the individual planetary influence and of the strengths of the differing aspects. It is important to mention that these planets are not lined up on one side of the zodiac in an astronomical sense but that they are so astrologically speaking.

There is a difference which would take a long time to explain.

If, for example, a stellium were to begin in the last few degrees of Aries but also spread in to the early part of Taurus, then the subjects of both signs should be advised to be aware of what is going to happen. In this way, the people concerned could look forward to an interesting time but, whether it is going to be good or bad, at the very least it is going to be an intense and very sensitive period.

How such an event may affect individuals is not always possible to fully explain. However, if anyone has anything special planned for such a period they are advised to create some alternative arrangements – just in case!

The two stellia in early 2021 suggest that Aquarians will need to look to their laurels and be prepared for some interesting times. For the most part, I feel that both events will be largely beneficial, although the January stellium placing of Mercury and Jupiter here implies whatever does happen will depend on how the individual identifies with people. Therefore the folk in their circles will probably want the Aquarians and themselves to become interested in something new. Be advised that these two short spells of concentrated power will also affect Virgo people with a tad more tension than usual.

The stellium on March 28 2025 will be helpful to Aries folk who want to better themselves and take advantage of people and events as they occur. However, the Moon position suggests much will depend on the mood of the moment with few diversions to take their minds off the target. Leo folk who won't take kindly to any opposition in normal times will be even more so. Facts, not ideas will matter here.

The Jan 17 2026 positions will help status conscious people but it will be necessary to watch for those who are skilled at fraud, forgery or just plain conning activities. Nevertheless, with most of the stellium planets placed in late Capricorn, even they may well have a hard task getting what they want. Cancerians are a canny lot as a rule and they won't stand for any nonsense. They are also very difficult people if or when anyone is fool enough to try to put one over on them.

Major Conjunctions

From time to time, when two or more of the outer planets come together, especially in conjunctions, it often signals very important changes or events, for individuals or society as a whole. Obviously, much depends on the house or sign in which this event takes place. You will have already read what may be in store for you in your personal sign forecasts for the next ten years but astrological events like this always help to put the icing on the cake.

In the coming ten-year period there will be small number of these events starting with Jupiter square Saturn on Jan 17 2021 in Aquarius followed by Saturn square Uranus on Feb 17 also in Aquarius.

When the first event occurs avoid hasty decisions and try not to be too obstinate either. Virgo folk are likely to want to or will actually end some relationships without thinking things through properly. Gemini may well not be so "hail fellow, well met" as usual, while Scorpio subjects could blank everyone out on sight – they can be so unpredictable at times.

In 2024 a Jupiter/Uranus conjunction occurs in Taurus on April 21. Ambitious folk everywhere will be seeking more power and status for themselves or for those whom they are able to "control". Leo people will be a tad more intense than usual. This could have quite an effect on people and organisations of all kinds. Severe changes are likely and among them is a strong possibility of civil war not only in the UK but in other countries as well.

Almost two years later in 2026 on Feb 20 there will be another conjunction between Saturn and Neptune but this time in Aries. Leo folk might be inclined to be apparently more amenable than usual in order to get their own way but they may also be down in the dumps for what seems to be no real reason. Taurus and Scorpio subjects will probably be hard to deal with while this influence is in effect.

In 2027 on April 12 Saturn and Uranus become semi-square in Aries. Saturn is not happy in this sign and coupled with a Uranus conjunction, expect sparks to fly just when you least expect them. So much could go wrong for no apparent reason at this time.

There will be a Saturn Pluto square in 2028 on June 24 in Taurus. The stubborn attitude of Taureans is well known and this influence is not going to help them much. There may well be some innovations in the music and or art worlds. This looks as though it might be a curious short period when freedom loving folk could end up crossing swords with those who are the exact opposite.

Jupiter will be opposition Saturn in Taurus in 2030 on April 24. For many, the rule will be "what's yours is mine and what is mine's me own". Uranus is unhappy here, while Saturn incites people to possess more and more – whatever the cost. Take care, everybody!

The benefits or otherwise of serious events like this don't happen that often but when they do, it would be wise to make plans accordingly.

Money

Astrologers must lose count of the times they are asked if someone will come into money, win it or inherit it. And, once again, it is the personal chart that must be carefully screened for such matters. But, there are ways in which we can learn to time personal financial affairs to best advantage.

In your personal birth chart, the second and eighth houses are largely concerned with how and when these times would be the most favourable. The fifth house normally shows the best time is to have a small flutter or a serious gamble.

What follows is **not** a fool-proof method but it does indicate the most propitious times to become involved in financial matters. When the Sun is in your own sign or the one immediately following then that is the best time to invest, purchase or to save money. The times the Sun is in any of the signs should be easy to find out because most newspapers tend to start their daily astrological forecasts with the current Sun-sign.

The Signs of the Zodiac

The most generally accepted dates for the entry of the Sun into each of the signs are shown here:

SIGN	ENTRY DATE
Aries	21 March
Taurus	20 April
Gemini	21 May
Cancer	22 June
Leo	23 July
Virgo	23 August
Libra	23 September
Scorpio	23 October
Sagittarius	22 November
Capricorn	22 December
Aquarius	20 January
Pisces	19 February

So, if you are an Aries subject then the most favourable period for you is between 21 March until 20 May and for Taurus folk, between 20 April and 21 June and so on until we arrive at Pisces, which would be between 19 February and 19 March of any year.

When joint money matters, income, investments, savings or possible inheritances are concerned note when the Sun is in the 8th sign from your own. This is the best time to deal with these kinds of financial affairs. For Aries folk, this would be the sign of Scorpio, between 23 October and 21 November; for Taurus, when the Sun is in Sagittarius, between 22 November and 21 December, and so on until we arrive once again at Pisces, when we should wait until the Sun is in Libra, between 23 September and 22 October of any year.

Of course, it may not always be possible to wait for such a moment but, if an opportunity to make a profit arrives within this time framework as outlined for you, then seize the moment, because the stars are in your favour.

Love, Sex and Romance

Love, sex and romance are usually at the top of most people's list. "When will I fall in love, enjoy sex or start a romance?" are often the first things astrologers are asked. As a rule, it is not a question of will so much, as when. Once again, we should look to the natal chart to get clear indications of the possibilities but there is a way around that – in general terms. The most romantic times for anyone are when Venus and Mars are passing through their own Sun-sign.

Venus

When Venus is in your sign, you seem to gain that extra special inner glow about you. The ladies pay much more attention to their appearance to attract romance with a better ease than at any other time. The same goes for the men, for they also smarten up their appearance to look good and dress well to attract romance.

Venus is in your own sign at least once a year and it varies from year to year and, when it is five signs away you may well begin to enjoy a new romance that could lead to love and marriage. However, when Venus is seven signs away is the best time to begin a partnership with a view to a long-term commitment, pop that special question or actually marry.

Mars

When Mars is in your sign, the same glow is there, but your sex drive and passions are never far from the surface and sex and romance will be on your mind. The ladies seem more amenable, more coquettish, inviting and ready for physical love and romance. The men appear to adopt a manlier stance and are quickly noticed by women. It is almost as if both sexes are aware of what may or may not happen although, astrologically speaking, they do not know why.

Mars is in your own sign at least once every two years. It varies from year to year but when it is five signs away then the sex drive will be very strong. To meet anyone now can easily lead to a blazing affair few people experience in the whole of their lives. When Mars is placed seven signs away is a great time to cement any existing relationship with a view to marriage.

Venus and Mars

On the basis of what you have just read, it obviously follows that if or when both Venus and Mars meet in the same sign, not only is it the most favourable period for you and or your present partner it must be one of the best times to enjoy love, sex and romance.

At such times, partnerships can become quite physical. No account is made as to who the partners may be or, indeed, of their age. It can be a legal or an illicit affair where the couple concerned may be from any walk of life or relationship. This is often the time when "eternal triangle" affairs can both start or finish – especially if or when they become public knowledge.

At these times, young people in their teens may well experience their first sexual encounters as they are caught up in their first love. Passion is the driving force at such times. Obviously, these occasions do not happen often but when they do occur they are unforgettable and they tend to live in the memory for many years.

I have listed the positions of Venus and Mars in the table of times and dates for when Venus and Mars meet in the same sign during the next ten years from 1 January 2021 through to 31 December 2030 for the reader to experiment with as he or she chooses at the time (*see opposite page*).

These rather potent periods become even more so when Venus and Mars are in your own Sun-sign, or five or seven signs away. Should the planets meet in an Air or a Fire sign, it favours all the Air and Fire sign people. If these two planets meet in an Earth or Water sign then romance will favour Earth or Water sign subjects.

CHAPTER TWENTY

Inner Planetary Places

These are the times when Venus and Mars are in the same sign between January 01 2021 and December 31 2030.

Odd days here and there are not included.

YEAR	FROM MONTH	TO MONTH	SIGN
2021	JUN 02	JUN 11	CANCER
	JUN 27	JUL 22	LEO
2022	JAN 24	MAR 05	CAPRICORN
	MAR 06	APR 05	AQUARIUS
	APR 15	MAY 02	PISCES
2023	MAY 03	MAY 23	CANCER
	JUN 06	JUL 09	LEO
2024	JAN 23	FEB 12	CAPRICON
	FEB 17	MAR 11	AQUARIUS
	MAR 22	APR 05	PISCES
2025	NOV 30	DEC 15	SAGITTARIUS
	DEC 24	JAN 17	CAPRICORN
2026	JAN 23	FEB 10	AQUARIUS
2028	JUN 07	JUL 09	GEMINI
	AUG 08	SEP 04	CANCER
	SEP 05	OCT 01	LEO
2029	SEP 10	SEP 23	SCORPIO
	OCT 07	NOV 04	SAGITTARIUS
	NOV 06	DEC 13	CAPRICORN
2030	JUN 22	JUL 02	GEMINI
	JUL 17	AUG 11	CANCER
	AUG 15	SEP 04	LEO

Outer Planetary Places

These are the positions of the five outer planets calculated from January 01 2021 through until December 31 2030.

JUPITER

YEAR	MONTH	SIGN
2021	JAN 01	AQUARIUS
2021	MAY 13	PISCES
2021	JUL 28	AQUARIUS
2021	DEC 29	PISCES
2022	MAY10	ARIES
2022	OCT 28	PISCES
2022	DEC 20	ARIES
2023	MAY 16	TAURUS
2024	MAY 25	GEMINI
2025	JUN 09	CANCER
2026	JUN 30	LEO
2027	JUL 26	VIRGO
2028	AUG 24	LIBRA
2029	SEP 24	SCORPIO
2030	OCT 22	SAGITTARIUS

SATURN

YEAR	MONTH	SIGN
2021	JAN 01	AQUARIUS
2023	MAR 07	PISCES
2025	MAY 25	ARIES
2025	SEP 01	PISCES
2026	FEB 14	ARIES
2028	APR 13	TAURUS
2030	JUN 01	GEMINI

URANUS

YEAR	MONTH	SIGN
2021	JAN 01	TAURUS
2025	JUL 07	GEMINI
2025	NOV 08	TAURUS
2026	APR 26	GEMINI

NEPTUNE

YEAR	MONTH	SIGN
2021	JAN 01	PISCES
2025	MAR 30	ARIES
2025	OCT 22	PISCES
2026	JAN 26	ARIES

PLUTO

YEAR	MONTH	SIGN
2021	JAN 01	CAPRICORN
2023	MAR 23	AQUARIUS
2023	JUN 11	CAPRICORN
2024	JAN 21	AQUARIUS
2024	SEP 01	CAPRICORN
2024	NOV 19	AQUARIUS

Glossary of Terms

Terms used in astrology can be confusing to a newcomer at first. Some astrological terminology is extremely ancient but is used as a matter of course by astrologers without thought. It is for this reason a glossary of terms will be found helpful.

AIR SIGNS
The so-called mental or intellectual signs – Gemini, Libra and Aquarius.

ANGLES
The four main points of the chart are the ascendant, mid-heaven, nadir and descendant – the cusps of the first, tenth, fourth and seventh house respectively.

APPLICATION
The approach of one planet to another as it begins to form a recognised aspect. When they are in the proper position, the aspect is said to be exact and, as they move away from each other they are called departing aspects.

ASCENDANT
Also called the rising sign, this is more properly the actual degree of the sign of the zodiac on the eastern horizon for the date and time given for the birth or event for which a chart is constructed. It is the most important point in a horoscope and the point from

which an astrologer will begin his assessment of character and personality. He will also refer to this point when he comes to calculate future events.

ASPECTS
The measurement of angles, in degrees, between the planets or the planets and points of the chart are known variously as major or minor or easy or hard. These are calculated by dividing the full 360 degrees of the zodiac into recognised angles. The major planets are the conjunction, square, trine and opposition – 0, 90, 120 and 180 degrees respectively. There are many minor aspects of which, perhaps, the most well-known are the sextile, quintile, and quincuncx – 60, 72 and 150 degrees apart. There are many more; among them, midpoints, which are the exact halfway, or midpoint between aspects often found to exert an influence in a chart.

ASTEROIDS
Small planetoids usually found between the orbits Mars and Jupiter. The five used most are Ceres, Chiron, Juno, Pallas Athena and Vesta. Not all astrologers use them, while others may use more of the lesser known – it is left entirely to the individual astrologer.

BIRTHCHART
One of the many names for a horoscope, of which others are: nativity, natus, map or wheel. It does not follow that a chart is necessarily for a birth. A map can be constructed for any event or time – past, present or future.

BST
British Summer Time or daylight saving time is a feature common in most countries. Lists of these time changes for the UK and other countries are published separately.

CARDINAL SIGNS

Aries, Cancer, Libra, or Capricorn are the Cardinal Signs. They are called this because they mark the changes of the seasons and are the first sign of that season. These personalities usually possess good initiative.

CUSP

This is an astrological term for the dividing line between the signs or the houses in a chart for a person or an event. Cusp babies are those born on the immediate either side of this dividing line between the signs.

DEGREE

The zodiac circle is divided into twelve signs of 30 degrees each. Each degree contains 60 minutes and each minute holds 60 degrees of longitude.

DIRECT (MOTION)

Planets are said to be direct when moving forward or as they begin to move from a stationary position.

ECLIPSE

Solar and Lunar eclipses are very important astronomical events that have special astrological meaning within the framework of birth chart analysis and assessment of potential events.

ECLIPTIC

Often said to be the Sun's apparent path in the heavens, but better expressed as the path the Earth travels in its annual journey around the Sun.

ELEMENTS

The signs are divided into four elements, fire, earth air and water. The fire signs are Aries, Leo and Sagittarius; the earth signs are Taurus, Virgo and Capricorn; the air signs are Gemini, Libra and Aquarius and the water signs are Cancer, Scorpio and Pisces.

EPHEMERIS
This is a publication that list planets, their places and other astrological and astronomical data.

EXALTATION & FALL
In astrology, exaltation is one of the five essential dignities of a planet. Each of the older planets is exalted (or is said to rule) as follows:

Sun:	Aries	the three newly discovered planets are said to be exalted as shown
Moon:	Taurus	Uranus: Scorpio
Mercury:	Virgo	Neptune: Sagittarius
Venus:	Pisces	Pluto: Aries
Mars:	Capricorn	planets in FALL are the opposite signs
Jupiter:	Cancer	to their exaltation
Saturn:	Libra	

FIXED SIGNS
Taurus, Leo, Scorpio and Aquarius are the Fixed Signs. People who belong to these signs tend to be fixed or stubborn in their ways.

GMT
Greenwich Mean Time, This is the universally adopted time system throughout the world. Time zones were created to correct for the difference in clock time at Greenwich based on the longitude of the place under review.

HOUSES
There are twelve houses in a birth chart that equate roughly to the twelve signs of the zodiac. The system by which an astrologer arrives at house division varies greatly and according to the astrologer concerned. The most universally employed is Equal House. The other most used systems today are Koch and Placidus. There are many others now widely fallen into disuse.

LATITUDE

Geographical measurement noted from north or south of the equator outward to the poles. Latitude may be termed north or south if the place under review is north or south of the equator. Celestial latitude refers to a planetary position north or south of the ecliptic.

LONGITUDE

Geographical measurement east or west of Greenwich measured by degrees, minutes and seconds. Celestial longitude is measurement along the ecliptic from the first point of Aries.

MIDHEAVEN

The highest point above the horizon of the chart in question, in some cases the cusp of the tenth house. Also known as the Medium Coeli and usually written as Mc for short in a birth chart.

MUTABLE SIGNS

These are Gemini, Virgo, Sagittarius and Pisces. People from these signs tend to be fairly easy-going.

NADIR

The lowest point below the horizon of the chart in question, in some cases the cusp of the fourth house and always exactly opposite the Mc.

NOON CHART

Quite frequently people either do not have their time of birth or do not know it with any accuracy so a chart showing the planets for noon is created. If the subject feels they may have been born earlier in the day, a map for dawn or 06.00 may be drawn. Similarly, if they know they were born much later in the day, a chart for sunset or 18.00 hours can be made up.

OOB PLANETS
When a planet is "Out of Bounds" (OOB) its declination exceeds 23° 28' north or 23° 28' south. It is then regarded as having "escaped" the constraints and physical space dominated by the gravitational "boss" of the solar system – the Sun. The planet is said to be away or out of control and no longer has to observe the rules – it is considered to be free to do as it pleases.

PROGRESSIONS
A chart produced for as many days after a birth as the subject is in age and used for ascertaining possible future events. There are a number of different ways of calculating such charts but, unless the time is known to within four minutes, any predictions deduced could be up to a year wrong. Transits are far more widely used these days.

RETROGRADE
This is the period of time when a planet appears to be moving backward through the heavens as seen from the Earth. Some astrologers take the view that this is a special event, while other may ignore the phenomenon altogether. It is a matter of personal choice for them.

STELLIUM
A collection of planets, usually more than four, in one sign or house in a birth chart. If it is spread over two houses then allow no more than 20° of arc. These events can be very significant events and do not occur very often.

SIDEREAL TIME
This is solar or astrological time and, using this method, a day is reckoned at 23 hours, 56 minutes and 4 seconds. It differs from standard clock time by about 4 minutes each normal or civil day.

SUN SIGN

This is used to refer to people born during the passage of the Sun through a sign. Thus, for example, someone born when the Sun was passing through Cancer is said to be a Cancerian, or a Sun-Cancer subject. If born when the Sun was passing through Libra, then they are a Libran, or a Sun-Libra.

TRANSIT(S)

The daily movement of a planet used to compare its present position with that of all the planets and points in the original or radical birth chart. This is the most accurate way of assessing potential future events and can be used even when the original chart has been prepared without reference to a time of birth.

VOID OF COURSE

This is the name given to the Moon when she moves past the last traditional or accepted aspects to when she enters the next sign. She is said to be neither one thing nor the other at such a stage. This period may last for just a few minutes or can be as long as 28 hours. This may happen several times during any one calendar month. Planets can also be called v-o-c during the course of a month.

ZODIAC

The area of sky divided into twelve signs about 8° on either side of the ecliptic. It is also known as the tropical zodiac and is different to the Sidereal Zodiac that uses the constellations of the stars.

ZONE STANDARD

The standard time zone used in different countries that will be behind GMT or ahead of it, depending on where they are. Their time will need to be converted to GMT before an accurate horoscope can be created.

www.ingramcontent.com/pod-product-compliance
Lightning Source LLC
Chambersburg PA
CBHW061310110426
42742CB00012BA/2134